A COUNTRY DOCTOR

IN THE SOUTH MOUNTAINS

by BENJAMIN EARLE WASHBURN

ILLUSTRATOR · JOHN PIKE

THE SPINDALE PRESS

SPINDALE, NORTH CAROLINA

To

R<small>OBERT</small> W. M<small>C</small>K<small>AY</small>, M. D.

Whose generous nature, innate skill, and thorough training have
enabled him to bring happiness to his fellow-man.

Foreword

The stories told in this narrative are true; however, in some instances a number of related happenings have been combined to avoid repetition. Names of persons and families have been changed, although there can be no reason for anyone to feel embarrassed because of the part he or his family played in the life of a wonderful community which existed in the South Mountains country fifty years ago.

• • •

The drawings which illustrate the narrative are by John Pike, N. A., to whom I am much indebted for the interest he has shown in this account of life in the mountains of western North Carolina at the beginning of the present century. He is well acquainted with the section and has drawn inspiration for many of his paintings from the scenery and people of this part of the country which has been one of the final strongholds of early Americanism.

CLEVELAND COUNTY

WEST KNOB

N

NO BUSINESS MT.

BLACK MT.

AARON BUMGARTEN

BRIAR CREEK

BOOSEY KANIPE

FIRST BROAD

RICHLAND MT.

BIG HUCKLEBERRY

LISENBE PEAK

LITTLE HUCKLEBERRY

BURKE COUNTY

HARDBARGAIN CREEK

SKIFF GADDY'S BRANDY ORCHARD

FIRST BROAD CH.

FIRST BROAD P.O.

SALLY QUEEN CREEK

HOSEY HOUSER

SOUTH FORK

PR JULI

SKULL KNOB

FIRST BROAD RIVER

BIG JULE SHELTON

WEAST PEAK

NOLANS KNOB

LONE MT.

MARLIN PEAK

CA

McDOWELL COUNTY

TO MARION   DYSARTSVILLE

RUTHERFOR

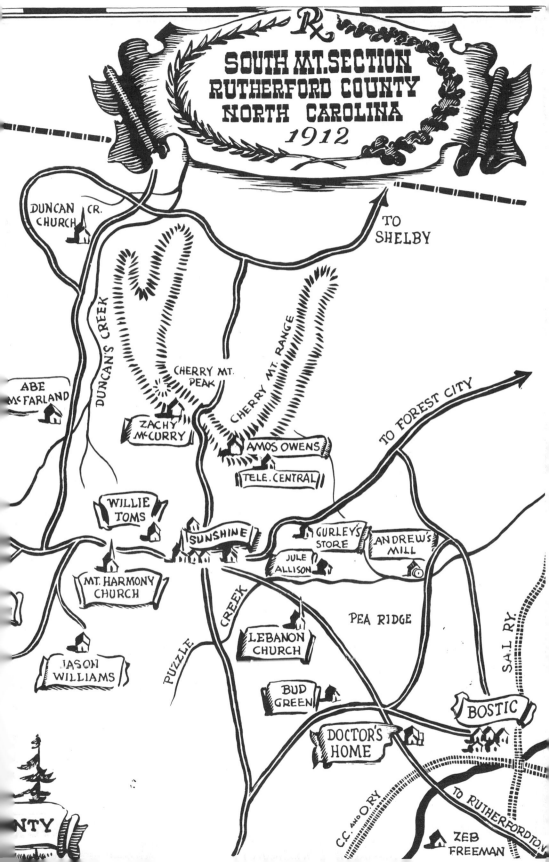

"In Golden Valley typical mountain homes of logs were encountered."

In the South Mountains

MY medical career began with fourteen months of general practice in the northern and mountainous section of Rutherford County, North Carolina. It was by invitation that I located in these foothills of the South Mountains, and looking back after a lapse of about forty years I believe that in many ways these fourteen months were the most interesting I have experienced. It all came about in this way. Being without funds after finishing my hospital internship, I had no choice except to locate in my home town of Rutherfordton although the place was well supplied with doctors. I established an office and practiced there for a month. This month, February 1912, was cold and rainy and the few calls I received were from patients whom the other doctors were reluctant to visit, since they lived in inaccessible places or were chronics who had no means of paying their bills. The unimproved roads of the county, hub-deep in red mud, made travel by horse and buggy very slow and difficult. At the end of the month it was necessary for me to borrow money to pay my bill of $20.00 for room and board at the Southern Hotel. I was thoroughly discouraged.

But on March 4, I was visited by a delegation of more than a dozen men from the upper section of the county. They represented the communities of Mt. Vernon, Brittain, Pea Ridge, and Mt. Lebanon in Logan's Store Township, and Sunshine and Golden Valley in the South Mountains. They came to invite me to locate in their part of the county, explaining that Dr. Thomas Avery, who had practiced there for many years had recently retired and moved away, and they were looking for a doctor to take his place. A large country practice had already been built up, they said, and there would be no end of medical work from the start, in case I should move there. One of the men from Golden Valley assured me that I'd "get ter ride over the mountains ever' night". But more to the point, Bud Green, who had bought Dr. Avery's home place, offered to provide board for me and my horse at a very reasonable rate and to allow me the free use of Dr. Avery's former offices. Needless to say, I moved to the district on the following day.

The delegation was correct in saying that there would be calls from the time I located in the district. Within a fortnight I had enough work to keep me busy and some of my patients paid cash at the time of the visit. In addition to this desirable circumstance, I found the

9

people kind and hospitable and was struck with the fact that living conditions were quite different from the ways of life in the part of the county in which I grew up. This was particularly true of the rough South Mountains country. It seemed to me that to go from the lowland section of the county into the South Mountains, although the distance was only about thirty miles, was to pass into a different world— a world which showed stage-by-stage changes in civilization which had been going on in our Appalachian hills since the early years of the nineteenth century. It was easy to observe that the customs and living conditions of the people changed and became more primitive the farther they lived from the railway. In the rolling country about Bostic and between that place and Brittain, both near railways, there were passable roads and the homes were of modern design, but the type changed as you went into the hills. Box houses and small farms predominated beyond Sunshine Gap, while in Golden Valley typical mountain homes of logs were encountered.

Being young and of a romantic turn of mind, moving into this mountainous district caused me to picture myself as living and working in a country which presented a pageant of Middle English civilization, such as I had gathered from my study at the State University of the period from Chaucer to Shakespeare. And as I became better acquainted with the people I found it hard to realize that the South Mountain folks and those of the lower part of our county were largely descended from the same English and Scotch immigrants. This was all the more interesting since I was related to many of these mountain families, one of my grandmothers having come from this section.

2

People of the South Mountains

THE South Mountains in North Carolina comprise minor ranges which branch eastward from the main Blue Ridge and extend for nearly forty miles to form the boundaries between McDowell and Burke Counties on the north and Rutherford and Cleveland Counties on the south. They are typical of the smaller Appalachian ranges, being rugged and cut into gorges by water courses which, as they pass into the foothills, are surrounded by small fertile valleys. In 1912, the South Mountains presented a formidable barrier between these four counties, so much so that most travel went east or west around the mountains, instead of by the rough direct roads which were impassable even to wagon traffic in rainy weather.

The district in which I practiced extended on the south from two railway lines at Bostic to Burke County on the north; and I had calls which carried me into all four counties. My home and office was at the Pea Ridge Cross Roads, six miles northwest of Bostic and five miles from Sunshine, a small village beautifully located at the foot of Cherry Mountain Peak and at the entrance to the gap leading into the South Mountains. The district was thickly populated and I soon came to realize that most of the families were related either by birth or marriage. And their dialect and superstitions were interesting, as was also the fact that there were a number of older women who sang "love ditties", as they called the current ballads of the hill country, although the singing of these was frowned upon by the church folks. But above all, I was interested in the diseases of the South Mountains and the remedies employed in the system of folk medicine which had grown up in districts rarely visited by a doctor.

Within a radius of three miles of my home there lived twenty-three families of Freemans and in the range of my practice there were numerous families of Longs, Andrews, Logans, McFarlands, Campbells, Morrisons, Morgans, and Graysons, while the Sheltons seemed innumerable. Many of these people bore identical names, and to differentiate them the given name of a boy or girl or wife was often added to that of the father or husband. Bill Jack Grayson, for example, was Bill the son of Jack Grayson; while Mary Ringgold Freeman was Mary, the wife of Ringgold Freeman. Then there were a number of men with the same name who were distinguished by the adjectives "Big" and "Little", such as Big Willie and Little Willie Long (Big Willie owned

11

a store, while Little Willie was a farmer); Big Sam and Little Sam Biggerstaff (in this case, Big Sam was a man small in stature who owned a sizeable plantation, while Little Sam, a giant of a man, had but little property); then there were Big Mike and Little Mike Freeman, Big Pink and Little Pink Hardin, to mention a few others; also, Red Andy and Black Andy Higgins, so named from the color of their hair. When it came to the Sheltons, there were Big Julius and Little Julius, Thousand Dollar Julius, Preacher Julius and his son, Little Preacher Julius, Horse Trading Julius, and a number of others.

•   •   •

The South Mountain people have an interesting history. Their forefathers were the protestants who were planted in Ulster by King James I during the early years of the seventeenth century. Later, losing favor with the English Crown they likewise lost their leases on land in Ireland and this caused them to migrate to America, where they settled in Pennsylvania. From Lancaster County, Pennsylvania, many moved to eastern North Carolina where they hoped to find better land and a more equable climate — and they were always in search of religious liberty and personal freedom. In eastern Carolina, however, they found conditions no better than in Ulster. The fertile land had already been taken up by large plantations which, worked by slave labor, supported a wealthy aristocratic class. They soon found that a meager living was all that could be eked from the poor upland farms on which they were forced to settle. The more adventurous, dissatisfied with such conditions of life, moved west into the Appalachian country where land was plentiful, even if it was rough; and in the sparsely settled mountains individualism could be practiced to each family's satisfaction.

In this mountain country roads were hard to build and there was little communication between different sections. As a result, each family was confined to its own locality and knew little of the outside world. Two hundred years of this isolation developed a people who still lived in the eighteenth century. They had become so accustomed to the hills and primitive ways of living that they were adverse to making changes; they still retained the ideas and customs of their ancestors and developed an intense individualism and a passionate attachment to their homes. This attitude was expressed by many of the South Mountain people in their dislike of the lowland country and especially of South Carolina; and I am told that this is true of mountain people in all the North Carolina counties along the southern state line. Many of these families had gone to South Carolina to work in cotton

12

mills and, invariably, they had become homesick and moved back to the hill country.

Since the First World War the entire mountain country has been face to face with change. The important sources of water power and the abundant timber and mineral resources found in the region began to be developed. And every year isolated districts have been reclaimed. In the South Mountains hard-surfaced graded roads have been built, post-offices and mail routes established, schools have been erected, and modern ways of living have been adopted. With the coming of telephones, electricity, and automobiles all but the most isolated homes have been brought into closer touch with the present-day world. As a result, much poverty and ignorance and misery have undoubtedly been removed, but, on the other hand, a picturesque section with simple, loyal, homeloving families has been lost. And this is a loss which involves the ability of families and individuals to live self-contained lives, finding happiness in following traditions inherited from past centuries and other countries; which excellent qualities, so much needed in our present-day civilization, have vanished never to return. It is this background which made the fourteen months I lived and worked in the South Mountains the most interesting period of my entire life; and it has made me recall most vividly the friends and acquaintances I made and the incidents with which I was associated from March 1912 until May 1913.

3

Local Diseases and Remedies

EARLY in my practice I learned that the usual point of view as regards health was that everyone is more or less ill — and in this they were fairly right. If a man were asked about the health of his family, more often than not he would tell you that he himself is "tolerable" or "jest middlin'"; that "the ole 'oman is ailin' as usual"; and that one or more of the "chaps is right puny". Dyspepsia was found in almost all adults and children, being caused from eating thick soggy corn pone or half-cooked wheat bread, with greasy vegetables, and too much salt pork. Bad sanitary conditions, or a total lack of any kind of sanitation, existed at practically every home and, as might be expected, typhoid and the diarrheas, and other bowel ailments were common. Other complaints were "pneumony fever", "side pleurisy", "joint rheumatism", "jumping toothache", the "bloody flux", and the "gallopin' consumption", to give the more descriptive designations of well-known diseases.

There was an outbreak of milk sickness ("trembles") among the cows during the autumn I was in the region, with two cases of "milk sickness" among the people. This is the disease that is said to have killed Nancy Hanks, the mother of Abraham Lincoln. It was caused by cows eating poisonous weeds, according to popular belief, though at the time I never found anyone who knew the particular plant that brought on the condition. The disease is really serious and may prove fatal to the cow or to human beings who drink her fresh milk or eat the fresh butter; but I was told that the disease is not transmitted by buttermilk. The symptoms are a violent digestive upset with nausea, vomiting, and great weakness. The local treatment was an emetic, followed by a purge, and frequent doses of brandy and honey, which treatment was as good as any I knew. There were a number of interesting beliefs regarding milk sickness; milk from a sick cow was said not to foam and that a silver coin would turn black when it came in contact with the milk. I was unable to verify either of these reports. Many mountain people, especially the older ones, had a strong aversion to milk and butter and refused to eat either. Fear of milk sickness may have been the cause, for I was told that the disease had been much more prevalent a generation before than at the time I lived in the district.

A complaint with many children as well as adults was "dew

"A complaint with many children as well as adults was 'dew-p'izen', characterized by slow-healing sores on the feet and legs."

p'izen", characterized by slow-healing sores on the feet and legs and often on the hands and arms. At the time I did not recognize "dew poison" as the preliminary stage of hookworm disease nor did I associate it with the stunted anemic condition of the mountain children. The absence of privies at the homes made the disease very prevalent and there is no doubt that it was responsible for much of the ill-health. I have often regretted that I did not recognize the presence of hookworm infection among my patients.

Digestive upsets in babies and small children were said to be due to "growing down of the liver", whatever that may have been. Skin eruptions of all kinds, especially when attended with fever and fretfulness, were ascribed to the "hives", a condition carefully watched for fear it might turn into the "bold hives". "A good doctor can cure the hives if he gets it in time, but it takes a monstrous good un' ter cure the bold hives", I was told on more than one occasion. As can well be imagined, fatal cases of scarlet fever and other childhood infections were often ascribed to "bold hives". The old remedy for the condition was to scarify the baby over the left shoulder blade, collect a drop of blood in a silver spoon and give it to the child by mouth. This procedure had already been replaced by calomel and senna tea before my advent to the community.

Crude obstetrical work was an important cause of ill-health among the women. The mountain midwives were without training and many of them were old and ignorant; and not only was there lack of cleanliness at confinements, but there abounded superstitious practices which were harmful to both mother and baby. During labor the woman was often "sneezed" with snuff to hasten delivery, and not infrequently this resulted in perineal tears. Then immediately after the child was born the practice was to make the already exhausted mother blow into an empty bottle to bring about the expulsion of the placenta. After this the hips were held together for at least half an hour by pressure from either side "ter push the hip bones back inter place", for according to the explanation given me for the procedure "they mos' allus come oncoupled".

The mountain people were easy to teach and were eager to adopt any new method of living the advantage of which has been demonstrated to them. Among the results of my fourteen months' work in the district, I have been especially pleased to think that I was able to bring about marked improvement in obstetrical work. The women were quick to recognize the benefits of cleanliness and to note the decrease of childbed fever as well as the more rapid convalescence in cases where the superstitious practices of the midwives were not employed. I also met with some success in teaching mothers how to take care of their babies; I especially denounced the practice of feeding a new-born baby on "pot-licker", the local name for the water in which vegetables had been boiled, during the first four days of life or until it was possible for the mother to nurse it. Also, I denounced the practice of rubbing whiskey on the baby's head before the cord had been cut.

Other things I advocated with varying degrees of success were better methods of nursing the sick, the value of fresh air in lung troubles, the avoidance of noise and the exclusion of crowds from the sick room. How these reforms were brought about will be told further on when I describe the treatment of patients who came under my care.

• • •

It did not take me long to acquire a profound respect for the herb remedies employed in the treatment of disease and as first-aid agencies, and, also, for the men and women, usually elderly persons, who gathered and cured these herbs and were versed in their use. Of course, some remedies were pure hocus-pocus, but there was real virtue in many of them. An example was the common home remedy to stop bleeding from cuts and bruises. This consisted of gathering leaves from three different trees or bushes, bruising them thoroughly by rubbing between the hands, and then binding the mass to the wound. This proved effective in injuries where an artery was not involved, because all leaves contain a varying amount of tannic acid; if the leaves are gathered from three different trees it is more than likely that leaves containing enough of this astringent to stop the bleeding will be collected. Some herb gatherers claimed the remedy was more effective if the leaves were gathered in the "name of the Father, the Son, and the Holy Ghost".

Another and better example was the treatment of burns. Burns were quite common in the mountain homes since the cooking was usually done in open fireplaces. The skirts of women and children often caught from the unprotected blaze and serious burns were encountered. The accepted treatment was to wash the wound and dress it with clean cloths soaked in an infusion made by steeping oak "balls" (galls) in water. These oak galls were gathered in the late summer and autumn by anyone who happened to find them as he walked through the woods. They were cut into small pieces and made into the infusion which was stored in bottles for future use. If I had been more observant, I would have noted and, perhaps, reported on the effectiveness of tannic acid in the treatment of burns several years before it was announced to the medical profession.

Still another and more surprising example of the knowledge of medicinal herbs was encountered in the treatment of facial paralysis. When I first saw the patient, about two weeks after the paralysis occurred, he was already on the road to recovery. His treatment had been a tea made from the roots of "black crowhop". I recalled that a recently suggested treatment for facial paralysis was *Tr. Cimicifuga racemosa.* To obtain this drug a prescription would have to be sent to the nearest drug store, in Forest City, more than twenty miles away. Since the patient was improving under the local treatment, I decided not to change this. Upon returning home I consulted my materia medica and found that the common name of *Cimicifuga* is Black Cohosh and that it grows in the North Carolina mountains. Later I secured a specimen of "Black Crowhop" and found it to be Black Cohosh.

Makers of Moonshine Liquor

BY FAR the most common medicinal agent in use in the South Mountains was whiskey, nearly always in the form of "white corn" made in blockade distilleries; and it was fairly cheap and easy to obtain. At the time, strong sentiment existed in the district against the enforcement of the law forbidding the manufacture of whiskey without a Government license. Many of the most respected citizens were in open defiance of the law, honestly believing that anyone had an inherent right to raise corn and make it into liquor if he desired to do so. These men, by openly defying the law, encouraged others to engage in illicit distilling because it was profitable. At the time I lived in the district two operators of such stills had gained much notoriety. These were Amos Owens and Skiff Gaddy.

Amos Owens was known throughout Rutherford and adjoining counties. He had taken an honorable part in the affairs of the county during the Civil War and Reconstruction, and since that time had been a regular attendant at the criminal sessions of the Superior Court. I remember having seen him when I was a boy, when he came to town on court days. He was a small man, clean shaven, and always dressed in a long Prince Albert coat, and he wore a shining high beaver hat. Many tales were current regarding his experiences as a blockader on Cherry Mountain where he had his home, especially of the manner in which he outwitted the revenue officers. His house was built of stone on a spur near the top of the mountain overlooking the valley towards Sunshine village. He had a telescope with which he could keep an eye on the single rough road leading through the valley and across the mountain. With this he could spot a traveler a full half hour before he reached the gap. The house had three stories: on the ground floor Amos kept his mules, the family lived on the second floor, while the top story was given over to keeping bees. There were a number of bee "gums" in a large front room through which one had to pass to enter the back room where Amos was reputed to store his liquor

Cherry Mountain, as would be inferred by its name, was, before 1900, covered with cherry trees, though none could be found there twenty years later. The cherries usually ripened during the first two weeks of June and this was the time that Amos made his annual run of cherry bounce. On the second Sunday of June crowds of people from Rutherford, Cleveland, and Burke counties would visit Amos to buy cherries and drink cherry bounce. The beverage must have been potent for, too often, this second Sunday of June became the occasion of drunken brawls and bloody fighting. This was one of the reasons why Amos was so often either a defendant or a witness in court. He seemed to enjoy these appearances, however, especially the notoriety he gained by his witty replies to questions from lawyers and his success in evading justice. On charges of distilling he was taken to the Federal Court in Charlotte, and he had been there so many times that he became well-known to Judge Boyd and other court officials. On one of his early arraignments he begged the Judge to deal leniently with him, explaining that it was his birthday and, also, the anniversary of his wedding. It happened that this was also the Judge's birthday as well as his wedding day, so he asked for details and found that he and Amos had been born on the same day and that they had identical wedding dates. Amos was let off with a suspended sentence.

Years later, and a few months before I moved to the district, when Amos had become an old man, he was again brought before the Federal Court. The judge called him up and gave him a lecture, saying something like this:

"Amos Owens, your record shows that you have been convicted on a number of occasions for illicit distilling and that you have served several sentences in the State prison. You are now an old man, nearly 80 years old, and I don't know what to do with you. There is no need of sending you to prison again; you are not able to work and being confined to jail would likely be injurious to your health. If I should dismiss the charges against you and allow you to go home, what would you do?"

"Your honor", replied Amos, "I'd start a run of corn liquor the day I got there".

The judge meditated, and then continued: "I'll tell you what I'll do. Your partner, this young man, will have to be sent to the penitentiary for two years; as for you, I'll suspend judgment in your case if you'll agree to leave the State."

"I'll take an appeal!" exclaimed Amos. "It's a miscarriage of justice — sending one man to the penitentiary and making the other go to South Carolina".

Again, Amos was let off with a fine and a suspended sentence.

•   •   •

As to Skiff Gaddy, he lived beyond Golden on the North Fork of

20

Sally Queen Creek; his apple orchard at the junction of the mountain roads was a landmark, directions being given with reference to "Skiff's Brandy Orchard". Although I heard interesting accounts of Skiff's encounters with revenue officers, I never saw Skiff. At the time I was in the district he was away in the State penitentiary at Raleigh; not, as would be supposed, for illicit distilling, but for disturbing religious worship.

Caring for the Sick

THE spirit of helpfulness, especially for those in difficulty, is a dominant trait of the North Carolina highlander. In fact, the trait was often carried to extremes in the South Mountains in the care of the sick; and one duty of the doctor was to protect his patients from the over-zealous care of friends and relatives.

One of my early calls was to visit Mrs. Zachy McCurry, whose husband, a well-to-do citizen, had his home on Cherry Mountain on a ridge fully 1000 feet above the surrounding plateau. This was beyond the village of Sunshine and about ten miles from my home. I had never been up on Cherry Mountain and was surprised when I was told that the trip could be made by buggy. The road beyond Sunshine was steep and rough and I saw no houses or signs of life as the horse climbed the pass and on to the top. As I drove along I could not help but think of my patient, who I was told was more than seventy years old, and of how unsatisfactory is the treatment of serious illness in an out-of-the-way and desolate mountain district. One of the difficulties of medical work in the mountains was the impossibility of seeing patients at frequent intervals, no matter how ill they might have been. The distances were too great, the roads were too rough, and the people were too poor to pay for more visits than were absolutely necessary. Because of these things the doctor was never called except in cases of serious illness and often when the patient's chance of recovery is past.

It was past the middle of the afternoon when I reached the top and found the usual mountain home of the better class. In the front yard was a large square building of one story and with one large room, on three sides of which were shed rooms built of rough lumber. The front door opened from a wide porch into the main room which contained the large stone chimney and wide fireplace and served for both a sitting and a bedroom, while the side rooms were unheated bedrooms. At the rear of the yard was a similar square log house; in this the large room was the dining room and the shed rooms the kitchen and pantries. Further back were a number of small buildings, the barn, stables, cribs, and other out houses. As a mountain family increases or when the boys marry and bring their brides home, buildings similar to the "big house", but perhaps of a smaller size, are often erected in the same yard with the home of the old folks. There were two such buildings in Zachy McCurry's yard.

I was led into the "big house". The large open fireplace, at least five feet wide, held a blazing log fire which lighted the entire room; the small paneless windows on either side of the chimney had their shutters tightly drawn to keep out the chilly air. About the fire were old Mr. McCurry, a son, a daughter, a son-in-law, and six grandchildren. The patient was in one of the three beds which were at the back of the room. She had been ill for about a week and examination showed that she had lobar pneumonia.

My treatment consisted of a mercurial purge, strychnine for the heart, and a cough mixture; along with fresh air and rest in bed. The drugs would be administered correctly, I felt, since one of the sons-in-law, Randy Jenkins, could read and write and could be depended upon to follow the directions. But there was opposition to the most important part of the treatment. The patient, I ordered, was to be moved to a side bedroom which was not tightly built and had a large window. Mountain folks are unusually free from lung diseases because their houses are open and fresh air is plentiful; but when such diseases do occur the cause is always ascribed to fresh air. So marked is this belief that quilts were often hung around the high bed posts to keep as much air as possible away from the patient.

So it was no great surprise to me that the patient and her family hesitated to make the changes I suggested. In the end I thought it best to compromise and the bed was moved to a corner between the main door and a door leading into a side room, after I had secured a promise that these doors would be left open.

It was on Thursday that I visited Mrs. McCurry and I arranged to see her again on the following Sunday. Other calls would make it impracticable for me to come earlier unless I should receive an emergency call, which was to be sent in case of a serious turn in the patient's condition. With this understanding I descended the steep pass and went further into the hills to visit other patients.

As was often the case, when paying a prearranged visit into the hill country beyond Sunshine I found calls awaiting me from other sick folks in the same neighborhood. In fact, it was necessary for me to spend the night in the district. On Friday morning, at Sunshine, I heard that Mrs. McCurry was much worse and was not expected to live through the day; that a telephone message had been sent to my home during the night and that a messenger had gone into the hills in search of me. I was told that the patient was weak from persistent vomiting, following the medicine I had administered.

It was a relief to learn the nature of her sudden setback, for the mercury might have been the cause of her nausea which in all probability had passed off by this time. But I was urged by one of her relatives who lived at Sunshine to go again at once to see Mrs. McCurry.

On reaching the house, I found her much better, with an active skin and somewhat lower fever, though she was weak from the purge. I was told the nausea lasted for more than two hours. I reminded them that they had been told to give sips of hot water in case there should be nausea. They had forgotten this and the patient had not been relieved until one of the neighbor women made her some "writing paper tea". I had never heard of this remedy but a Mrs. Robbins volunteered to tell me how to prepare it properly. This valuable remedy she had learned to make while working at a cotton mill in South Carolina. It is a simple recipe: take a sheet of "white note paper which costs a penny over to Sunshine and which has never been wrote on"; place this in the bottom of a pitcher and pour boiling water over it. Give it to the patient while hot. I promised to return on the following Monday; but a messenger was to bring me news of the sick woman on Sunday.

This messenger came and said the patient was much better as far as her fever and weakness were concerned, but added that she had not slept since I had first seen her and at times she was delirious. This caused me to plan a visit on Sunday afternoon instead of waiting until the next morning.

I had much urgent work to do and it was dark before I reached Sunshine where one of the McCurry boys awaited to guide me up the dark mountain road. We discussed his mother's condition. I could not account for her sleeplessness and realized that this would soon cause the patient's condition to become serious and that she would require careful nursing. I asked if there were neighbors willing to help with the house work and the care of the patient.

"Oh yes", replied the boy, "our neighbors are mighty good ones and are always helping us."

"But are there any who live nearby who could sit up at night if it is necessary?"

"Oh yes", was again the reply. "They're real good erbout that. There wuz thirty-five set up with us last night; in fact, Ma's bedroom wuz plum' filled with 'em."

"My God!" I exclaimed as I realized the cause of the patient's nervous condition. "It's no wonder the poor woman can't sleep."

After this I wasn't surprised to find the room filled with men, women, and children, together with a number of crying babies. After

24

"One of the McCurry boys awaited to guide me up the mountain road."

examining the patient I took old Zachy aside and told him that he must put everybody out of the room except two who were needed to look after his wife. He agreed and sent a boy to build a fire in one of the nearby houses before he sent us to the dining house for supper.

When we had eaten and returned to the patient the young folks had moved off reluctantly to the yard house but there were still eighteen people in the room. All the mothers and babies remained. The old man hesitated as he told me he couldn't carry out my orders; the older folks thought they should stay with the sick, and he couldn't hurt their feelings.

So I took the case in hand and asked brutally if they wanted to murder the sick woman. Then I selected two women to stay with Randy Jenkins and sent the others away. It was easy to see that my talk and actions were resented, as some of the neighbors went off home and the kinfolks stood outside muttering. I remained for more than two hours, until Mrs. McCurry had been given a warm bath and had gone to sleep.

As I was getting into the buggy, Randy Jenkins came out: "Say Doc", he asked, "can't yer change Maw's med'sin' er bit? It is giv' ever' two hours; an' they've kep' me up night an' day fer the past four days a-readin' d'rections, an' I'm all in! I allus puts the bottles on the table an' shows 'em which ter give when the clock strikes the next hour. But jest as I gets to dozin' off they wakes me up, since they's afeared some of the chaps or neighbors may hev' mixed the bottles or something. It's bin the same thing over an' over an' bein' able to read has sure bin a fair calamity on me."

I ordered the room to be kept quiet and Mrs. McCurry allowed to sleep until she woke of her own accord. No drugs were to be given until I came again.

Eighteen hours later I found her without fever; she had slept more than twelve hours and was on the road to recovery. Provided they did not hold a crowded thanksgiving meeting in her room there were not likely to be relapses. As I was leaving old Zachy came out to the buggy with me:

"Doc, I thinks you treated this case exactly right; you certainly treated her to my liking. Some of the boys think you talked mighty rough to us last night an' it's likely hurt some of the neighbors' feelings. But, Doc, I believes you saved Mandy's life."

26

The Hard Lot of a Tenant Farmer

IN THE Southern United States, during the first quarter of the present century, the life of a tenant farmer was a hard one; and this was especially true in the mountainous sections where the land is hilly and unproductive and the tenant had to put up with bad housing conditions. Often the tenant family was a victim of circumstances. Because of illness or other mishap their small farm, often inherited, may have been mortgaged; bad crop years may have followed and the home been lost. And, once a tenant always a tenant was almost invariably the rule. One-third to one-half of the crop had to be given for rent; bills for clothing and foodstuffs, usually supplied by the landlord at exorbitant prices, had to be paid; also, accounts for fertilizer and tools had to be settled, to say nothing of medical bills.

Jule Allison was such a tenant farmer; with a large family of eight children, wife, mother, and mother-in-law there was little hope of Jule ever being able to recover his small ancestral farm at the foot of Carson Mountain. Years before I knew him he had moved over on Puzzle Creek in order to be near a school and on a good road. Hard work, honesty, loyalty to family and friends, patience, and perseverance availed nothing in his case; his large family was prone to sickness and disaster. And even in good crop years medical bills took any surplus which may have been saved from the living expenses of the family.

I had been living on Pea Ridge for only two weeks when I had a call to go to Allison's home. My friend Green, with whom I boarded, was enthusiastic over the call.

"You 're goin' ter be a success, Doc", he commented. "I can see that. If yer can get Jule's an' Zeb Freeman's an' Plato Rollins' docterin' ter do, you can make a good livin' outer them an' all the rest'll be profit. Some er Jule's folks air down all the time an' Doc Avery uster go thar night an' day. An' Jule's rale good pay even if he is pore as Job's turkey. I was sorter a-feared Jule might call a Forest City doctor. He has so much docterin' in 'is family that all the settlement usually uses the doctor he gits. Anyway, Doc, they'll all have their eyes on you."

It was a little girl that was ill, Jule explained to me when I reached his home.

"The baby's right poorly with the bloody flux. I kno' I sh'u'd er sont on fer you sooner, but after Doc Avery went away from our country Carrie, that's my wife, said we'd try an' git erlong 'thout so much docterin'. She tho't Avery come too often jest beca'se we allus tried to pay him all we owed 'im ever' fall."

"How long has the child been sick"? I asked.

"A-goin' on ter ten days now", he replied. "When it fust took down, Miss Lawter, she's Carrie's Ma, made it some slippery elm bark tea; but that didn't do one bit er good, an' 'sides it made the little chap vomit. I wanted ter send fer you right off, but Miss Lawter said I gathered the bark the wrong way. She says if you scrape it offen the tree down'ards its good fer bowel complaints, but if you scrape it up'ards it causes vomitin' right off an' so's good fer a sick stummick.

"Well, Miss Lawter gathered some bark herself, but all the time the baby kep' gettin' wuss. I kno' it ain't exzactly right ter call you in after the little chap's so weak an' all, but, Doc, it's the only little gal we's got an' Carrie'd be powerful put out ef it sh'u'd die."

The child, I found, had acute dysentery and was weak and emaciated; and she did not readily respond to treatment. It was easy to recognize the truth of Bud Green's assertion that the "settlement" had their eyes on the new doctor. The house and yard would be filled with people from nearby homes at the time of my daily visit. And I was stopped along the road to answer inquiries about the sick child.

A week passed and the baby was no better. In fact, she was weaker and more emaciated and I could see that the community had come to the conclusion that death was inevitable. Jule, I was sure, would be held responsible for the loss of the child since, in the eyes of his neighbors, he should have known better than to entrust the baby to a new and unknown medical man. But Jule was the soul of loyalty. I suggested a consultation.

"Hit's fer you ter decide, Doc", was his reply. "I kno' you've done all that c'u'd be done. If we sont off ter town fer a doctor, it'd take 'im a long time ter come an' he c'u'dn't stay more'n er hour when he got here. He c'u'dn't l'arn much in that time. Onless you air of a min' that ernother docter can holp you. But I kno' you've done all you can do. 'Sides, we didn't sen' fer you soon ernuff, tho' the women folks seem ter've fergot that."

I returned to the sick room which was crowded with visiting women who sat about the hearth talking in subdued tones while they dipped snuff. I was struck by the large number of flies about the sick child's bed. For the first time, for some reason, I connected the condition of the room with the illness of the child. On two occasions there had been improvement in the patient's condition; but each time, after

28

two days, there had been a set-back. If my diagnosis of bacillary dysentery was correct, and I was sure of it, these relapses had been due to reinfections. I called Jule outside and asked to be shown the privy.

"The privy", he hesitated, "you mean the back-house? Why Doc, we ain't got none. Big Willie Houser half promised ter build us one when we fust rented this place from him, but he's never done it an' I ain't never been able ter buy lumber; an' anyway, none o' the neighbors has sech a thing."

"Have any of you had bowel complaints before now?", I asked.

"Yes", he replied, "some of us seems ter be down with the flux most of the time. An' one o' the boy chaps had the bloody flux 'bout two months ago."

"The germs which cause flux", I explained, "are often spread by flies. I have just come to the conclusion that flies have brought germs to the baby and given her the disease over again each time she got better. Do the women boil the child's soiled clothes, as I instructed them to do?"

"Miss Lawter looks after that an' she b'ils 'em ever' day. But she piles 'em out behin' the barn an' the flies may get to 'em afore she 'tends to the b'ilin'."

Investigation showed this to be the case and steps were taken to prevent further reinfection by flies; a net was secured for the baby's bed, care was taken to keep flies from the food, visitors were excluded from the sick room, and within a week after the inauguration of this new regime the child was on the road to recovery.

"Thar ain't ernother doctor in the county that c'u'd 've saved that little chap", was Jule's comment. "I never hear'd of any doctor warnin' erbout flies carryin' the flux; leastwise, they never said enything erbout it. An' I been thinkin', Doc, if we'd had a back-house an' kept flies outer the house the baby w'u'dn't need ter 've had the flux at all, nor any of the boy chaps neither."

Uncle Jason Williams – Herb Doctor

LONNIE Blanton's baby had the thrush or "thrash" as the condition is called in the South Mountains. The inside of its mouth was so covered with the characteristic small, white, furry ulcers that the baby couldn't nurse without pain. I asked the mother how long the mouth had been sore and what treatment she had used.

"Well, I 'spects its mouth's been sore now endurin' a month, but it ain't been cryin' bad more'n erbout a week. We's tried ever'thing, but nothin' seems ter do airy bit of good. Fust, we hearn that passin' a baby back'ards through a white mule's collar was good fer the sore mouth; but it didn't help our child any that we c'u'd tell. Then ernother remedy we learned of is ter git a stranger, who you've ne'er seed erfore, an' have 'im give the baby a drink of spring water outer the brim of 'is hat. But we live so fur offen the main road 'at we ain't seed a stranger pass yet; so we ain't tried that remedy."

"Yes", I broke in, for I was exasperated, "but haven't you thought of washing the baby's mouth? Thrush is caused by not keeping the mouth clean."

"Lar', no", she answered, "we war' tol' 'at water'd made it wuss. In fac', Uncle Jason Williams, who's my great-grandpap, said it w'u'd make it spread. An' Uncle Jason has a mighty good repertation with babies throughout these parts. He hearn erbout our little chap bein' sick an' come ter us yestiddy, 'g'inst night."

"Well, what did he tell you to do?"

"Why, ain't you hearn erbout Uncle Jason, how he's a seventh son an' how he can blow in the mouth an' cure enny trouble whatsoever of the mouth and throat whether the sick pusson is a chap or a grownup?"

"But why did you send for me if your grandfather has already treated your baby?" I asked.

"Hit's all beca'se of Lonnie. He growed up in the low country an' never hearn of our home remedies. Nothin' w'u'd do but he mus' up an' sen' fer you 'thout waitin' ter see what vartue there war' in Uncle Jason's breath."

I had just finished preparing a mouth wash for the baby when Uncle Jason came in. He was an old man, tall and erect, and intelligent-looking. He wore a long beard and gray hair which reached to his shoulders.

"Doctor, the baby's got a fair touch of the thrash, ain't 'e? Lonnie here w'u'dn't give me a chance ter use my powers on the baby. I ain't no doctor but I's l'arned a deal endurin' the eighty-five year I been goin' up an' down the yarth."

"Mrs. Blanton tells me that you treat mouth and throat troubles by blowing in the patient's mouth. I'd like for you to tell me about this."

"Yes, Doc, it's this way. Only a seventh son has sich a power; an' a seventh son of a seventh son has still more 'raculous powers. My maw was a seventh gal, an' that gives me the power. It's er inborn gif' which is 'herited."

"Is blowing in the mouth your only method of treating the sick?"

"By no means, Doc, by no means, an' I thanks yer fer the askin'. Fer one thing, take my remedy fer consumption. It was 'vealed ter me in a dream by the Angel Gabriel; an' it's a sure cure. Why, the Rutherford County Commissioners hev' give me permission ter sell it 'thout licenses 'ca'se it's sech er wunnerful med'sin'. But mostly I uses the yarbs an' roots of the fields an' the leaves of the trees fer the healin' of the sick, as directed in the Holy Book of Revelations. Why, Doc, thar's lessen half er dozen yarbs the which w'u'd cure all human ailments, if they wuz applied properly. You air er hospittle doctor, ain't ye?"

"Yes, I had hospital training after leaving the medical school", I explained.

"I s'posed as much; an' that bein' so I 'low you don't lay much store on the powers of a seventh son."

"No, you are right; I do not. In fact, I have been around the world quite a bit myself and this is the first time I ever heard of a seventh son possessing such powers", was my reply.

"Hit's jest as I 'spected", continued the old man, slowly shaking his head. "You don't read an' s'arch the scriptur's. Did I undersstan' yer ter say the yarth is roun'?"

"I didn't say so, but the earth is round; though I don't see what that has got to do with the powers of a seventh son."

"Well, if you'd s'arch the scriptur's daily, as we are enj'ined ter do, you'd know the yarth ain't roun'. Don't the Bible speak of the four

31

"Did I understan' yer ter say the yarth is roun'?"

corners of the yarth? It does. Well, how can anything have four corners and be roun'?" The old man appeared to be disgusted.

"But you needn't min' me at all", he continued. "Lonnie's thought it good an' well ter sen' fer you an' I'll not interfere with yore treatment. Don't meddle with other folk's bus'ness 'as always been a motto of mine. I intends ter start back ter my home near Mt. Harmony Church termorrer mornin' 'g'inst sunrise."

This was my first meeting with Uncle Jason Williams; but it was by no means the last. I had not yet learned the influence old men of his type possessed among the people of the South Mountains, especially as regards the treatment of the sick. Of course the baby got well, but the story of Uncle Jason's "cure" for consumption will take longer to tell.

The Cherry Mountain Telephone System

RURAL telephone systems became popular in western North Carolina about this time (1912) and community exchanges were established in many thickly populated districts. The Cherry Mountain Telephone System had just been installed in the South Mountains country. This "neighborhood telephone," as it was called, consisted of twenty or more "lines" radiating from the central office at Mr. Monty High's on Cherry Mountain. Each subscriber provided his own telephone and his part of the cost and work of putting up the wires and installing the instruments. The "center office" was run by "Ole man Monty's gals," and each subscriber paid twenty-five cents per month for central office service.

There were from twelve to twenty telephones on each "line"; so there had to be a variety of "rings" to differentiate calls to the different homes. One long followed by three short rings, for instance, called my home. Since every phone rang when any instrument on the line was used, the telephone was a convenient means of exchanging community news and gossip; and whenever a call was made every receiver on the line would be taken down and every home listened-in on the conversation.

A few days after my phone had been installed, I received my first call to visit the home of Big Willie Thornbeck. The telephone rang:

"Air the docter at home?" a voice inquired.

"This is the doctor speaking."

"Is that you, Doc? This is Big Willie Thornbeck's house and Big Willie wants you ter come an' see him right away. I 'low he's real sick from the way he's takin' on.

"You say — what's wrong o' him? He says ter tell you he's been er usin' of 'is new tellerfone too much an' the 'lectricity from it has upsot 'is nerves from head ter foot. I'll tell 'im you'll come afore nightfall."

• • •

During the week the central office opened I had been called to see Greenbury Hardin, who had moved his bed close beside the telephone so he might hear the conversation after he had retired and had gone to sleep with the receiver on his pillow. A thunderstorm came during the night; the line was struck and his telephone, not being properly installed, was wrecked. Greenbury was badly frightened and the shock made him deaf for a few days. But there had been no storm since and, as I drove to his home, I wondered what had happened to Big Willie Thornbeck.

He was in bed and appeared in a daze; at irregular intervals he would grind his teeth and his body would jerk and his muscles twitch. At first he was slow to answer questions, but he soon became talkative.

"Yes, Doc," he related, "the 'lectricity 'as got my nerves all on-strung. It come on gradual-like as I stood a-listenin' with my elbow restin' on the tall box and the black 'ceiver-thing to my ear. In fact, I could feel the lightnin' come in at my elbow and race up my arm and 'round my neck and into my head, and then go down the spine o' my back. Doc, is it real lightnin' what comes over the wires ter carry the talk?"

Examination showed nothing that would cause such symptoms; so I explained as best I could the mechanism of the telephone and ended by saying: "The small amount of electricity that you might receive from the telephone couldn't possibly do you any harm. In fact, your nerves must be in better condition than most people's nerves to detect any electricity at all. I have been telephoning most of my life and I never had any trouble like this."

"Yes, Doc, but you's been brought up on tellerfones and sich things but we South Mountain folks ain't usen ter 'em. Jest look what happened ter Greenbury Hardin. Warn't it 'lectricity what tore down 'is tellerfone and knocked hell out o' him besides?"

The patient gave a long yawn.

"How much of your time have you spent at the telephone?" I asked.

"Well, ter tell yer the truth, I can't egzactly say, but I 'low it's been a right smart bit."

"He's stood or sot at that 'air tellerfone fer forty hours han'-runnin'," broke in his wife. "I been tellin' 'im they ain't airy thing wrong of him 'cep' loss of sleep an' that he ought to be 'shamed of his-self ter pester you ter come all of ten miles with nothin' serious er ailin' of 'im."

The patient groaned as he said, "But Doc, shorely there's somethin' you can give a feller ter quiet 'is nerves. You can feel my pulse, how it races up an' down my arm, an' tell somethin' bad is wrong. I sont fer

"He's stood or sot at that 'air tellerfone fer forty hours han'-runnin'."

you ter get med'sin'; an' I mus' have med'sin', no matter if it were brung on by standin' too much at that 'air tellerfone."

I went out to my buggy medicine-case to look for a "nerve quieter." A top bottle was filled with pink "Infant Laxative - Mild" tablets, each containing one-tenth grain of calomel flavored with wintergreen. Two dozen were carried to the patient.

"Air these nerve strengtheners as well as nerve quieters?" he asked as I was preparing to leave. "Because I've spent out a matter o' 'leben dollars on this here tellerfone and it 'd be a fair calamity if I couldn't ever use it ergin."

Big Willie phoned the next day that he had slept well and was feeling much better. A few weeks later I received a letter with a one dollar bill enclosed from a man in an adjoining county. It read:

"Dear Sir: I am jest returned home from a visit to my cousin Big Willie Thornbeck. He gave me some of the pink nerve pills he got from you and I write to say that them there pills done my nerves more good than a hundred Dollar worth of nerve medsin I have used in the past four year and I am a person who frequents doctors. Enclose a Dollar bill for which please send me the worth of the same nerve pills and oblige, yours truly, Lum Vincent."

37

Pneumony Fever and the Side Pleurisy

BEFORE finishing breakfast one morning in April, I had a telephone call from Abe McFarland, who lived fifteen miles away on Duncan's Creek, beyond and to the south of First Broad post office. Abe 'phoned to say that he thought one of his boys had "the pneumony fever an' the side pleurisy both". I had not left home before I had another telephone call, this time from Little Preacher Julius Shelton. He also lived on Duncan's Creek several miles to the north of McFarland.

"Doc, can't yer posserbly come ter my house fust? I'd like it powerful if ye c'u'd". He spoke in a drawling, sing-song voice, which manner of speaking had caused him to be known as Little Preacher Jule to distinguish him from his father who spoke in the same way and was known as Big Preacher Jule. Neither of them, however, was a preacher.

"I'm very sorry", I replied, "but I have promised Abe McFarland to go there first. I will come to you from Abe's."

"Well, come on jest as soon as yer posserbly can. This is turrible weather we air havin' — hit's regular pneumony-breedin' weather."

At Sunshine, five miles from my home, I was stopped; someone wished to speak to me over the telephone. It was Little Preacher Jule.

"Doctor, I jest called yer ter l'arn how fur erlong you air on yore journey an' ter hurry yer erlong. An' say, Doc, couldn't yer try an' come ter my house fust, before yer go on ter Abe's?"

"No, I promised to go there first and I'm going as fast as the horse can carry me over these muddy roads. Goodbye."

Willie Toms lived four miles further on the road and had a telephone. He stopped me to say that Little Preacher Jule wished to speak to me.

"Doctor", announced Julius, "I called up Abe but Abe won't ergree fer yer ter come ter my house fust. I tho't I'd let yer know this in case yer might 've changed yer min' an' decided ter come on direct ter see us fust."

"Mr. Shelton", I replied sternly, "I'll get to your home just as soon as I possibly can, and much sooner if you don't stop me at every house where there is a telephone. It makes me fifteen minutes later every time I stop and telephone to you."

At First Broad post office the road divides, one fork going to the north and one to the south section of Duncan's Creek. Here I found a messenger from Shelton.

"I cain't tell yer what's the trubble over ter Little Preacher Jule's, but it mus' be somethin' powerful bad. He sont word ter Paw fer me ter come here an' tell yer ter come there before yer go ter Abe's; an' he axed Paw ter send one of t'other boys down ter Abe's in case ye went there fust."

It was noon before I was able to start for Shelton's. The messenger who awaited me at McFarland's had gone on ahead. About two miles on my road up Duncan's Creek, I met little Preacher Jule himself.

"I shore am glad ter know ye air on yore way ter my house. I wus a-feared yer might be delayed."

"Well, I am here at last", I replied. "But what in the world's wrong with you? I've had to stop and 'phone or jaw with some messenger from you every few miles. That's one reason I'm so late."

But the poor fellow threw up his hands.

"Doc, yer cain't imagine what a turrible time we air havin' over ter my place. The ole 'oman an' two of the gals air down, both grown boys air under the weather, an' the little chaps air barkin' like they 've got the whoopin' cough. To tell yer the God's truth, Doc, ever' last one on the place is sick 'cept Baxter, an' when I lef' home he wuz a-pukin'."

Only two members of the Shelton family were seriously ill. Cannie, a boy of fourteen, was in the early stages of pneumonia, while Gracie, an older girl, suffered from pleurisy. The boy was strong and healthy and the prognosis in his case was good. But the girl was frail and gave a history of previous attacks of "side pleurisy", had a chronic cough, and other symptoms suspicious of tuberculosis. I outlined my plan of treatment to the head of the house.

"There are two things that must be done if Cannie and Gracie are to have a chance to get well. First, you must see that they have plenty of fresh air — the more the better. And it's up to you to keep them quiet; by this I mean, you must not allow more than two persons in the sick room at the same time and no one must go in except the ones who are attending to the children. Do you understand?"

"Yes, Doc, but Uncle Jason Williams has already took a look at them chaps an' he say, jest like you, they have got the pneumony fever. But he says it's liable ter turn inter the typhoid erbout the fifth day if we don't put stewed ingun poul'ices on their chists. Is there any vartue in that?"

My reply was emphatic. "You have heard the directions I gave.

If you allow old Jason Williams or any of the others to smother the children in poultices or hang quilts around the beds to keep out the air or a dozen or more people to stay in the room day and night, they are almost sure to die. Now you can follow my directions or old man Williams', either one you like. But there are too many sick people in the country for me to bother with folks who won't follow my instructions. If you don't give them fresh air and a quiet room, you need not send for me again — there's no medicine I can give that will take the place of these."

"But, Doctor, yore treatment is so diff'runt from what we air usen to! But you've got a powerful good repertashun already in this country an' I'll try an' get 'em ter do as ye say. When do yer aim ter come back this way?"

"This is Tuesday", I said. "I'll return on Friday. I have so many patients I won't be able to come earlier. But that will be soon enough, for with fresh air and rest both Cannie and Gracie should get along all right until I return."

On my Friday afternoon visit, Little Preacher Jule was awaiting me at the barn. He was nervous and excited and his speech was more of a drawl than ever.

"Oh, Doc, I've been havin' a hell of a time since you were here. I tried, Gawd knows I tried hard, ter carry out yore d'rections, but the ole 'oman, an' the neighbors, an' Uncle Jason, an' Big Preacher Jule, who's my pap, an' all the rest 'lowed 'at fresh air w'u'dn't do fer them chaps endurin' this damp, drizzly spell. I tried my derndest, but Uncle Jason's my ole 'oman's grandpap, an' he's got a powerful good name fer pneumony an' chist trubbles an' he said ter mek' the room tight an' use the ingun poul'ices fer jest one day an' I'd sure see a change. All o' 'em were ag'in' me an' I c'u'dn't help but give in ter 'em."

"Do you remember what I told you; that I wouldn't be responsible for the children unless you followed my directions?"

"But Doc," he pleaded, "Gawd knows I tried ter do like you said, but what chance did I have with the whole entire Shelton an' Williams tribes erg'in me? You've been in these parts long ernough ter know us folks; don't go off an' leave me ter battle with 'em erlone. In case the chaps don't get well they'll be sure ter say I killed 'em."

I was sorry for the poor fellow, for I felt that he had tried to carry out my instructions. And I had learned of the influence of the old men and women of the South Mountains in questions of sickness and the treatment of disease.

"Well, tell me all that has happened since I was here on last Tuesday."

"I knowed you'd believe me, Doc, and that I tried, fer I don't want that either Cannie or the gal should die. You know that. After you left, I had ter 'gree ter the hangin' o' quilts 'roun' the bed an' the puttin' on o' ingun poul'ices, jest as I already told yer. But I 'greed fer jest one day; I sarved notice on the lot of 'em that if them chaps warn't a lot better in one day, they's have ter carry out yore d'rections.

"Well, neither of 'em slept one mite from the time they put the poul'ices on an' yestiddy Gracie were outer 'er head an' Cannie was weaker an' it were harder fur 'im ter breathe. An' they air still that way; tho' I think they breathe easier since I gin' 'em fresh air. But Doc, I've had a hell of a time keepin' the neighbors an' kinfolks outer that sick room."

As their father had reported, both patients were in much worse condition than when I had seen them two days before; in fact the girl's case was now hopeless. The boy was putting up a good fight, however. He had not been given a bath since the onion poultices had been removed from his body and particles of stewed onions were smeared over his skin. In the face of strong objections from Uncle Jason I gave him a warm bath and had his bed clothes changed. While I was thus engaged Uncle Jason called for his buggy and left for his home, saying that he would not stay and see the boy die as a result of the bath. But Cannie reacted well to the bath and went to sleep almost immediately.

I discussed the situation with Little Preacher Jule. Cannie had every chance of getting well but there was little hope for the girl's recovery. And, it was highly important that she should be removed into another room and away from Cannie.

"I was a-feared from the beginnin' that Gracie c'u'dn't pull through, fer years ago Doc Avery said she had the cornsumption", he said stoically. "But, Doc, air yer sure Cannie 'll make it? That's a bright boy an' it'd be a plum pity ef he sh'u'd go so young. And, Doc, you jest must stay an' see Gracie moved inter a next room."

It was long after dark when I left for home. By that time the girl had been moved and Cannie was still sleeping His fever had decreased and his heart was in better condition as a result of his bath and sleep.

• • •

Next day I was notified by telephone that Gracie died during the night. I started for Sheltons as soon as I heard this news for I was not

41

sure what would happen to the sick boy while funeral preparations were being made for his sister. As I expected, I found the yard and house full of people, for funerals are always largely attended in the South Mountains.

I had arrived too late. Cannie was in a state of collapse, with increased lung involvement, unusually high fever, and a failing heart. I was at a loss to know the cause of his collapse and questioned his father.

"Doctor, I know you 've done all that c'u'd be done an' it ain't yore fault 'at Cannie must go too. It were this way. After you left Gracie died, as you tol' me you was afeared she w'u'd do. I went ter take down one of the barn doors ter lay her out on an' when I come back inter the house, Cannie raised up in bed an' axed me if he c'u'd see Gracie after she were laid out. I axed the poor chap how he knowed anything was wrong with his sister an' then Doc I found out 'is ma'd told 'im she was dead. Well, Cannie kep' a-beggin' ter see her an' Uncle Jason, who'd come back by that time, said the boy was so sot on seein' 'is sister that we had orter bring 'er in so 'is mind w'u'd be relieved. So, after Gracie had been laid out we carried 'er on the barn door right up to Cannie's bed.

"Well, Doc, he jest raised up an' gin a long look at Gracie an' then he sorter swooned away an' from that on he's got wuss an' wuss. I reckon his bein' sick made 'im nervous-like when he seen Gracie. Anyway, we're waitin' erbout buryin' Gracie till tomorrow. If Cannie dies they can both be buried at the same funeral."

I could do nothing. The boy died three hours later.

10

South Mountain Dialect and Folk Music

IT WAS at Zeb Freeman's that I first became interested in the dialect of the people of the foothills and in the South Mountains, for it was there that I came to realize the relationship it bore to Middle English speech. Zeb owned an upland farm near Mt. Vernon church, south of Second Broad river, and he and his wife and eight children were among the most popular and respected families of the district. His wife, Cousin Dovie, a relative of my mother, could be depended upon at any time to help the sick and distressed of her neighborhood. On Sundays, after church services, Zeb and Dovie always brought friends home with them for the midday dinner. And if there happened to be visitors or strangers among the congregation, these were included in the invitation. And on Sunday afternoons and on holidays the Freeman home was the gathering place for friends and relatives, old and young.

Not long after I had located at Pea Ridge I was invited to dinner at the Freemans. The occasion was Cousin Dovie's birthday and the afternoon crowd of visitors was unusually large. The spring day was warm and we were sitting out under one of the large oak trees in the yard watching the children play; their game was called "The Happy Miller". This was played by a number of boys and girls, the boys always outnumbering the girls by one. They all formed in a ring and marched around, the boys going in one direction and the girls in the other; and as they marched they sang:

> "Happy is the miller who works in the mill,
> While the wheel goes 'round he works with a will,
> One hand in the hopper and the other in the sack;
> Now is the time to get your partner back."

At the end of the verse each boy catches the girl nearest to him and the extra boy who fails to get a partner is in the ring for the next round.

This song somehow brought back memories of the classroom of Doctor Thomas Hume at the University of North Carolina and the course in Middle English literature; and I recalled a line of an old dance, "Round and round, the mill goes round." Just then two small boys came running around the house and Zeb remarked: "Them tincey chaps are glib runners". From that moment I kept my ears open for unusual words and expressions, which I recorded in my notebook, as

I made calls and talked with the people. The following observations are taken from this notebook.

1.—There is a striking use of double words in description, some of the more common being: *cash money, sun ball, cow beast* or *cow brute* (bull), *church house, bare naked, fire hearth, play game, flower pretty,* and *rock boulder.*

2.—Many words are used with meanings no longer in general present-day usage: *awful*—meaning wonderful or awe-inspiring, as the telephone is *"an awful machine"; tincey* — little; *prancy* — gay; *smidgen* — small amount; *serious* — solemn; *welkin* — the sky; *trivet* — a wild person; *wastrel* — a no-account person.

3.—The weather is described by a number of words with varying shades of meaning; threatening weather is known as *falling weather;* mists are called *damping weather* or a *skiff,* also a *skiff of snow;* and a storm is a *tempest.* In describing a quarrel, *hardness* means ill-will; a *ruction* — an angry argument; a *rippit* — a fist fight; while a *fray* or a *fracas* is real fighting, with shooting or cutting with intent to kill.

4.—Among interesting expressions the following may be noted: *a penned at home woman* — a woman who stays at home; *a fine pretty morning; you hold him in talk* — you entertain him; *make me hear* — tell me; to be *forehanded* — to be saving; *who gave out to you?* — who told you?; *dad-burn* and *I gonnies* are swearing expressions; *a mite blinky* — a little sour; *'tain't worth the slavery* — not worth the labor; *his mouth ain't no prayer book; ever since his grandpap was panted; a sight in this world; in the smack middle of the day; mercy seat* or *anxious seat* — the altar of a church; *town fetched* — brought from town; *he's the banginest man* — he is a remarkable man; *it bangs my time* — it is hard to understand.

5.—The neuter form *hit* for *it* is not used except at the beginning of a sentence, or for emphasis after a pause.

6.—There are many peculiar verb uses: *to much* — meaning to pet; *to pleasure* — to entertain; *to ready* — to prepare; *to pretty* — to dress up. Strong and weak verbs are often confused, the strong forms being retained: *drownded; wopt* — for wept; *holp* — helped; *ruck* — raked. There is confusion of the past tense with the past participle: *he had went; they had not spoke; they had saw;* also, *I seen* and *they seen* are in general use. *I have run* is always used for the past tense. And *learn* is always used for *teach.* Also, there is no regularity in the use of the tenses and numbers of the verb to be.

7.—There is no regularity in the pronunciation of a number of common words; an example is the word *you,* which may be pronounced one of more ways in the same sentence — *you, yer,* or *ye.*

•　　•　　•

But going back to children's games, I made note of historic games, such as "King William Was King George's Son"; guessing games, like "Hull Gull", "Jack in the Bush", and "Thimble, Thimble, Who's Got the Thimble"; myth games, such as "Chicky, My Chicky, My Craney Crow" and "Old Grandma Hippity Hop". Work games were also popular among smaller children. Among these may be mentioned "This is the Way We Chop Our Wood — String Our Beans — Hoe Our Corn", etc. In these the singing was accompanied by gestures imitative of the work being done, which the other side would try and guess.

In discussing these games with me, Cousin Dovie Freeman remarked: "If you should ever get a call down on Duncan's Creek in the South Mountains, be sure and stop on First Broad and see Hosey (Hosea) Houser and his five old maid sisters. Elizabeth is a master singer of 'ballits' or 'love ditties', as some call 'em".

It was not long before I had an opportunity of visiting the Housers. Hosey ran a small store near First Broad post office, which was at the end of the star route which brought mail twice a week from Bostic into the South Mountains. He and his sisters were all musical, Elizabeth being the vocalist of the group, just as Cousin Dovie Freeman had said; and Hosey would accompany her on his home-made dulcimer. I was particularly interested in this instrument. It was usually picked like a banjo or a guitar, but could be played with a bow, like a fiddle, or with a quill, like a mandolin; and, finally, the strings could be tapped with a small hammer, as a marimba or xylophone is played. Elizabeth's favorite ballads were "Barbara Allen", of which she knew several versions; "Lord Lovell", to which local allusion had been added; "Fair Elinor", and "Lady Margaret". It was exciting to hear Elizabeth sing when it was recognized that her songs were versions of old English and Scotch ballads. Myrtie, a younger of the Houser girls, knew several more modern ballads, which she would sing while she played her guitar. Of these she liked best "The Dying Cowboy", "The Ship That Never Returned", and "Frankie Silver's Confession". The last-named was written by Frankie Silver while she was in jail for the murder of her husband and was recited or sung by her on the gallows just before she was hanged at Morganton in 1833. Also, Myrtie knew "The Death of Nellie Cropsey", a ballad based on a famous

45

North Carolina murder which had occurred some fifteen or twenty years back.

I became so much interested in these South Mountain versions of old English and Scotch ballads that I wrote Dr. C. Alphonso Smith, Professor of English Literature at the University of Virginia, about them. Dr. Smith had been my friend and former teacher at the University of North Carolina. At the time he was making a collection of ballad remains in the mountains of Virginia. Later, Dr. Smith wrote and asked for the address of the Housers and of others in the South Mountains who sang ballads. He was arranging an itinerary for Professor Cecil Sharp, of Oxford University, who was coming to the United States to visit the Blue Ridge Mountains and spend several months studying the folklore of the region. Professor Sharp made this visit and later published, with Mrs. Olive Dame Campbell of Brasstown, the results in "English Folk Songs from the Southern Appalachians", in 1917. He reported that the folklore of these Southern mountains was much more like that of Early and Middle English times than could be found in any part of Great Britain at that time. And he and Mrs. Campbell discovered and recorded a total of 122 songs and ballads, 37 of them being old English and Scottish ballads — many more than could be found in England and Scotland at the time.

11

Cousin Samanthy Grindstaff

RETURNING from a trip down Duncan's Creek one January day, I had stopped at First Broad Post Office to telephone. As I was going out to my buggy I was stopped by Hosey Houser.

"Doc", he called, "ef ye're in this section endurin' the next few weeks stop by our house an' see Cousin Samanthy Grindstaff; she's a-comin' ter take a month with us."

I accepted his invitation readily for I had heard of Samantha Grindstaff, who had the reputation of being the champion banjo player in the South Mountains. I asked Hosey more about her.

"Yes, Samanthy bears a great repertashun as a banjo picker an' I knows you'll delight ter hear her. Besides, she's quite a cha-racter; in fac' she's a sight in this worl'," he explained with enthusiasm.

"Where does she live?" I inquired; "and you say she's going to visit you for a month?"

"That's right, Samanthy pays long visits when she comes, but she's good company an' allus is welcome where'er she goes. An', Doc, she's one gallivantin' woman — furst here an' then thar. Rightfully, she belongs ter live with her paw up on One-eye Creek, jest erbove Skiff Gaddy's Brandy Orchard. But she visits with us erbout once a year, an' then goes on ter see her boy what lives down in Cleveland County; an' she's the great-aunt of the wife of one of Noah Bumgarten's boys, over towards Huckleberry Mountain, an' she stays with them part of the time."

"How old is she, and you say she has a married son?" were my next questions.

"As to her age," he replied thoughtfully, "that's something none of us knows. Some say she's in 'er seventies an' nigh on ter eighty — I jest don't know. An' since you ask, I might go on an' relate her history ter ye. As I say, she were raised over on One-eye Creek, an' when she was a young gal she run erway with Caleb Baily from over Bostic way. They was married an' had er boy; an' after he was a great big chap, she an' Caleb had a big ruckus an' she up an' di-vorced 'im, an' come back ter live with 'er paw. She fotched a banjo back with her an' changed 'er name back ter Grindstaff. An' she shore can pick that banjo. In fact, one year she took fust prize over ter Morganton at the big dance and music festival. Preacher Jackson Freeman don't approve of sech carryin'-on, an' her di-vorced, too, so at a big August meetin' held on upper Briar Creek, he churched Samanthy. This so riled 'er that she sassed the parson right out in public; an' then he withdrawed the hand of Christian fellowship from 'er. But all that didn't faze Samanthy nary bit an' she seems ter enjoy life jest as much as ef she was still enjoyin' full church fellowship. Now she visits ermong 'er kin an' 'quaintances, an', as I say, she's sech good company an' makes 'erself so useful erbout the house that we're allus proud ter see 'er come."

I was intrigued by this history of Samantha Grindstaff and made an opportunity to stop at the Housers' while she was visiting them. Samantha, to my surprise, did not look to be more than sixty, being a gaunt tall woman with a mass of gray hair combed tightly over her head. She had sparkling blue eyes and a smiling face and talked in a rapid manner, with a steady voice that was not at all like the slow drawl of her mountain neighbors. She certainly did not look like a woman who would "sass" the parson. As Hosey had said, she was a "banjo picker out of this world." She knew all the popular dance tunes of the South Mountains and many "ballit" tunes, among them a number about Jesse James. Her ballads were different from those sung by Elizabeth Houser, being of a more frivolous character. Whether such tunes were more suitable to banjo accompaniment or whether she selected them because she liked them better than the usual mountain ballads which were sung in slow, doleful tones, I do not know.

Two of her songs were easily recognized as new-world versions of old Scottish ballads. One of them, which Samantha called "Home Come Her Old Man," is a version of "Our Goodman," sung in Scotland in the early part of the eighteenth century. This ballad she introduced with an explanation that the man of the song had gone off on a drunken spree and got put in jail somewhere down in South Carolina. He was away from home for a long long time, perhaps a year, and the song tells of conversation between him and his wife upon his return. The man speaks first:

"I come home from my big spree,
  An' call my little wife ter come harkin' after me;
  My dear wife, my kind wife, my lovin' wife tell me
  Whose horse is in the stable where my horse ought ter be?"

"You poor blind fool, cain't you see,
  You son of a gun, says she,
  That's nothin' but a milk-cow
  Which yore mammy sent ter me."

48

"I've traveled erbout this world, —
  Gone a thousand mile or more;
  A saddle on a milk-cow
  I've never seed before."

"When I come home I call my little wife,
  And she come harkin' unto me;
  My dear wife, my kind wife, my lovin' wife tell me
  What's this hat a-doin' here, without leave o' me?"

"You poor blind fool, cain't you see,
  You son of a gun, quoth she,
  That's nothin' but a milkin' pail
  Which yore mammy sent ter me."

"I've traveled erbout this world, —
  Gone a thousand mile or more;
  But fur on a milkin' pail
  I've never seed before."

"When I come home an' call my little wife,
  An' she come harkin' unto me;
  My dear wife, my kind wife, my lovin' wife tell me
  Whose head is in the bed where my head ought ter be?"

"You poor blind fool, cain't you see,
  You son of a gun, says she,
  That's nothin' but a cabbage head
  Which yore mammy sent ter me."

"I've been traveling erbout this world, —
  I've gone a thousand mile or more,
  But whiskers on a cabbage head
  I've never seed before."

In the same manner a walking-stick is explained as a churn dasher, a wig as a setting hen, a man's coat as a blanket, a strange shirt as a table cloth, boots as coffee pots, and so on.

Another of Samantha's songs was a version of the old Scottish ballad "Get Up and Bar the Door." She called it "A Tale about Old John Jones and His Wife"; it went as follows:

49

One night the wind come out of the west,
Blowin' o'er the open floor;
Said old John Jones ter Jane, his wife,
"Get up an' shet the door."

"My hands are in this sausage meat,
An' I cain't get them free;
If you don't go an' shet the door,
It'll ne'er be shet by me."

They argued and they argued long
And 'greed when their talk was o'er,
The one who spoke the very first word
Should get up an' shet the door.

Along there come two huntin' men,
A-journeyin' in the night;
They come ter old John Jones' house
Beca'se they seen the light.

"O, does this house ter a rich man belong?
Or does it belong ter a poor?"
But never a world would old John say
Because of shuttin' the door.

The hunters bade, "Good evenin', Sir,"
When they looked in on the floor,
But ne'er a word would John Jones say
Because of shuttin' the door.

The hunters drank from the big black jug
That stood upon the shelf:
"Now since we've found a house of our own,
I'm sure we can help ourself."

An' then they ate of all the food,
Throwin' scraps upon the floor;
But ne'er a word did old Jane say,
Because of shuttin' the door.

Then says one man unto the other,
"You've got a good sharp knife;
You go an' shave the old man's chin,
An' I will kiss his wife."

"You've eat my meat an' drinked my ale,
But you'll not kiss my wife;
An' you'll not shave me," old John cried,
"Not upon yore life."

Then up there jumped old Jane Jones,
An' skipped across the floor;
"John Jones, you've spoke the foremost word,
So you must shet the door."

During my visits to the Housers I learned that this remarkable old woman not only played the banjo and sang ballads but also told folk stories which made her very popular among children. An example of these is the story of an argument which took place between the turkey and the duck over which could see daylight first. According to the story, the turkey claimed that he always roosted in the topmost branches of a tree and, naturally, could see daylight as soon as it became visible. The duck, on the other hand, contended that he had much better eyesight than the turkey and for this reason, although he roosted among the roots at the bottom of the tree, he could tell when day came before anyone else. Finally, after much talk, they decided to hold a contest, which the rooster was asked to judge.

On the night of the contest, the turkey flew to the very top of a large cedar tree and settled himself for the night. The duck, on the other hand, made his bed on the ground at the base of the tree. And the rooster took his place halfway up the tree, midway between the duck and the turkey. Soon they were all sound asleep and the night passed quietly.

Early the next morning the turkey in the top of the tree woke just as the first light broke in the east. In a low voice, he called:

"Duck, it's day! Duck, it's day!"

This woke the duck and he quacked in his loudest voice:

"Day! day! day!!"

So loud did he quack that the rooster, from his place in the middle of the tree, was awakened and, not having heard the low voice of the turkey, declared that the duck had been the first to see day.

51

12

Uncle Jason Williams' "Gilead Lung Balm"

"**M**ORNIN' DOC", Wister Biggerstaff called out as he hitched his horse. "There ain't none of us sick this time, thank Gawd. But I come ter see you erbout goin' up ter the Hamilton Quarters section ter see one of the Hemphill gals. She's been poorly ever since she come home from school over to Round Hill last fall an' ever' time I passes by goin' ter a place I rents erbove the Quarters I hear her cough an' cough an' cough somethin' dre'dful. It's some kinder lung trubble what ails 'er an' I 'spec's it's the cornsumption she's got."

"Are the Hemphills your tenants?" I asked.

"No". He shook his head. "They lives on their own place but they're dirt pore. Me an' my women folks 've been sendin' 'em eggs an' butter an' milk fer some time, fer the gal don't look like she gets ernough ter eat. But she don't seem to mend at all. I wants you ter go an' see 'er ter find if anything can be done fer her an' I'll pay yore bill."

It was another example of the willingness of the North Carolina highlander to help the poor and care for the sick. This spirit of helpfulness, along with hospitality, is a characteristic of practically every mountain family, no matter how poor and humble it may be. I knew Wister Biggerstaff was a hardworking man with a large family and that he was not able to meet his own bills, much less pay the doctor bills of others.

"I'll be glad to go on one condition", I answered. "The Hemphills are poor and need help; you are already doing your part. You keep on sending them food and I will supply the medical attention and whatever drugs the girl needs. It's just as much my duty to help them as it is yours".

Wister grasped my hand.

"It's sure good of you ter look at it that way, Doc. We knowed you'd be willin' ter holp, but as you air jest gettin' started an' pay is poor in this section, 'specially at this time of the year, the ole 'oman and me thought mebbe we sh'u'd pay the bill of the Hemphill gal, since we've knowed 'em fer so long."

• • •

The girl probably had tuberculosis, there could be no doubt of the diagnosis of lung trouble, but the condition was not too far advanced for recovery under proper treatment. She was a young woman, not much above twenty years, with an intelligent face, the pretty features of which were now drawn from her constant irritating cough. She had spent three years at Round Hill Academy, a normal school, about thirty miles away, supporting herself by work in the kitchen and dining room and by sewing. The strain of these years, with their overwork and late hours of toil and study, had been too much for her frail body and she had recently succumbed to the infection.

"Is there any hope for me, Doctor?" she asked in a plaintive voice. "I do want to live so much. I wanted to be a missionary, but I was so tired at the end of the term that I couldn't pass the examinations to enter college or to be a public school teacher either. But I know I can do good work here at home, over on Briar Creek or in the Huckleberry Mountains where there are no schools."

"There is no reason why you shouldn't get well", I replied. "There is no extensive involvement of your lung. The things you need and must have are rest, fresh air, sunshine, and good food; and you must keep from worrying. You need very little in the way of drugs, but I will see that you get all the medicine you need".

"But, Doc, there mus' be some kinder med'sin' that'll break up the cornsumption", broke in the girl's mother. "I've hearn of sech remedies. Besides we air very pore an' we cain't erford eggs an' butter an' cod liver ile an' the other things yer mention for Lizzie."

"Why, Mr. Biggerstaff told me he has been sending you eggs and milk and butter", I replied in surprise.

"They had to be sold for medicine", broke in the girl. "Mr. Biggerstaff has been good to us, but ma and all the neighbors thought I had to have drugs; the eggs and butter were sold and medicine bought with the money."

"What kind of medicine are you using?" I asked, turning to the old lady. "Let me see the bottle."

"It's Uncle Jason Williams' 'Gilead Lung Balm'," she replied as she handed me a large black bottle from the shelf. "It's got a powerful good name fer lung trubbles an' Uncle Jason come hisself an' seed Liz an' recommended it."

The bottle was half filled with a yellowish oily liquid which had the odor of pine rosin and a brackish, turpentinish taste. I could not decide what its ingredients might be.

"How much has she taken of this?" I asked.

"This air the sixth bottle. An' its right 'spensive. Uncle Jason

53

axes a dollar an' a half a bottle fer it, but he give us a special price. We 'greed ter buy five bottles an' he throwed in one bottle cost free. He said the six bottles orter carry 'er through".

"Well, it has come near carrying her through", I couldn't help saying. "Seven dollars and a half would have bought a large quantity of eggs and butter and other things which build up the body and help it in its fight against tuberculosis."

"But, Doc, there mus' be vartue in Uncle Jason's med'sin; the county has give 'im free licenses ter sell it, 'cause it air so valuable, he says." The old woman spoke in rather an indignant tone. Her daughter turned to her:

"Well, Ma, you know that medicine hasn't done me any good. I get weaker and cough more every day. I want to follow the Doctor's directions. If he and Mr. Biggerstaff will help me get well so I can work, I will repay them. And I do not intend to take another dose of that stuff old man Williams persuaded you to buy." She spoke emphatically.

•   •   •

Recovery was slow at first, but after a few weeks of rest and fresh air and sunshine, together with good food, there was decided improvement in the girl's condition. The benefits of proper treatment could be recognized and this brought cooperation from the family. Soon the doctor himself was amazed as he watched the manner in which the human body reacts against an infection.

54

13

The Angel Gabriel and the "Gilead Lung Balm"

THE bottle of Jason Williams' "Gilead Lung Balm", which I obtained from the Hemphills, I carried to Rutherfordton. I showed it to the Register of Deeds, who is Clerk of the Board of County Commissioners, and asked him why Old Man Williams should be allowed to peddle such a fake cure and take from poor people the money which should be used for buying food. And why, above all things, should he be given a free license to sell the stuff?

"It's politics, Doctor", he explained. "The old man came in here with a bunch of testimonials from preachers and others who said they had taken the medicine and been benefited by it. He even had a testimonial from an ex-high sheriff of the county. But the real reason he was given a free license is because he's an old Confederate soldier. The old boys always vote together and can get anything they want. The politicians are too much afraid of losing the old soldier vote to cross one of them."

"But, as I said, he's selling this worthless stuff for $1.50 a bottle and poor people with tuberculosis are spending their money for it instead of buying milk and eggs and food which would really help them. Isn't there anything that can be done to stop the old quack?"

"To prove his medicine is worthless, you would have to know how he makes it and what he puts into it. But I doubt if the Commissioners would stop him under any condition", was the opinion of the Register.

I was determined not to drop the case and sent a sample of the mixture to the laboratory of the American Medical Association for analysis. The report was that the mixture was a very complex one, containing among other ingredients, magnesium, sulphur, oil of turpentine, and other essential oils of pine distillation, together with traces of creosote and wintergreen. The method of preparation could not be determined by an examination of the liquid.

This was rather disconcerting; it was, of course, inconceivable that old man Williams, with no knowledge of chemistry or of drugs, could prepare such a complex mixture. I visited the old man at the home of his son, near Mt. Harmony church, but could learn nothing. He held to his story that the Angel Gabriel had appeared to him in a dream and given him directions for making the medicine.

Then I interviewed my friend Bud Green, who held a contract at the time for rebuilding a public road and had his camp about a mile from the Williams home. He promised to keep an eye on old man Jason in the hope of coming on him when he was preparing his medicine. A month went by and Green had nothing to report. But one night at the end of a rainy week, he came riding his mule at full gallop. I could tell by the tone of his voice that he had news.

"Hello, Doc", he shouted from the barn, "air ye gone ter bed? I's caught the ole fox at last, jest ergin sundown terday."

By this time he had tied his mule and was coming towards the house.

"Great", I exclaimed, "come right in and tell me all about it."

"Well, Doc", he went on, "hit war this way. As I promised I kep' my eye on the ole gent an' went over there ter buy eggs and sech like at all times o' day; an' I'd set an' talk ter Buddie an' the chaps an' w'u'd go all through the house. But thar' warn't a thing ter be seed an' I was 'ginnin' ter think mebby you was all wrong erbout what you think of the ole man's med'sin'. Well, you knows it's been a-rainin' fer erbout a week an' as I was comin' erway from seein' Buddie jest ergin sundown terday, I had ter walk through the field instead of 'roun' by the road on ercount of the mud. You know that thar' big pile o' sawdust whar' Eli Wilson had 'is mill when he cut the last set of Middleby timber erbout five year ago?"

"Yes, I remember seeing the big pile of sawdust. It's bigger than this house, isn't it?"

"Much bigger'n this house. Well, jest ergin sundown as I was agoin' by I seed ole Uncle Jason's figger on top of the pile right erg'in the sun ball. I thought at fust he was a-prayin', but he kept r'isin' up an' down, curious like; so I slipped up on 'im an' hid behin' the ole sawdust chute. When I got a good look at 'im I seed he was a-fillin' bottles wid the thick rosimy water what had settled in the sunk-in hole at the top of the sawdust pile."

"That explains the complex nature of the mixture he's selling", I exclaimed as I recalled the analysis given in the laboratory report.

"But, Doc, he adds some white stuff to it", Green continued. "He'd put in a han'ful of the white powder an' then pour a tin cupful of the rosimy water into the bottle on top of it, an' then he'd shake the bottle an' pour in more water. I waited till he war gone an' then I slipped up to the sunk-in place an' gathered up a little of the powder he spilt. I brung it erlong as I thought you might like ter see it."

He handed me a paper containing a whitish powder composed of small, odorless crystals. I tasted it; it had a cooling, saline, bitter taste.

"It's Epsom salt", I exclaimed.

"Wall, I'll be damned!" said Green. "The ole devil's been a-sellin' dirty sawdust water an' Epsom salts an' claimin' it 'ud cure the cornsumption. An' think of 'im a-gettin' a dollar an' a half a bottle fer the mess!"

The matter was reported to the Register of Deeds who was asked if the question of revoking old Williams' license should be taken up with the Grand Jury, or had it best be presented to the Board of Commissioners. The Commissioners took the desired action at their next meeting.

"No matter what the Doctor thinks, the med'sin' is good an' it war the Angel Gabriel who l'arned me how ter make it", was the comment of Uncle Jason Williams regarding the Commissioners' action.

"But did the Angel Gabriel tell yer ter add Epsom salts to it?" someone asked.

"No, I jest put that in myself, 'cause folks won't buy med'sin' what won't act on 'em".

14

Beyond the Huckleberry Mountains

THE greatest handicap to the practice of medicine in the South Mountains was the long distances over rough roads which had to be traveled to visit patients who were too poor to pay adequately. My practice extended into the mountains beyond Carson Mountain and Nolan's Knob and as far as the gap between the Huckleberry Mountains, a distance of more than thirty miles from my home, where the driving road ended. The people who lived "beyant Huckleberry" were poor and illiterate and few could afford the services of a medical man. In most cases acute illnesses did not receive medical attention and the patient died if he did not respond to local herb remedies. Chronic cases fared better; and where the patients were not too ill to be moved they were often brought to the Huckleberry Gap for a doctor to visit them.

The usual procedure was for the patients to stop at Aaron Bumgarten's home and remain there for the two or three days which were required for the doctor to reach them. The rural telephone system extended as far as Boozey Kanipe's, who lived four miles from the Gap, and at the time I lived in the South Mountains I could be called from there by telephone. The result was that my time of coming and proposed route of travel were known before I started and patients were brought from the hills to homes along the road where I could be stopped and interviewed.

My first trip into the Huckleberry Mountains was made in October and was full of interest. The call had come from Boozey Kanipe.

"Hello, Doc, how air ye? Could yer come over inter these parts in the nex' day or so? There's a woman here from beyant Huckleberry who's brought 'er little chap ter Aaron Bumgarten's fer you ter see. She ain't got but two dollars but I'll spread the news of yore comin' an' I reckon there'll be lots of others when they l'arn that you air headed this way."

I agreed to go on the following Sunday and asked what was wrong with the baby.

"Why, the woman says it's allus been runty an' that she thinks its liver's growed down. I seed it myself yestiddy when I was over to Aaron's an' it looks all wrinkled an' like a r'al oldish pusson when 'tain't more'n three year old.

"An' Doc", Boozey went on, "you'd better fotch erlong yore sounder an' take ernother lissen at my heart. It acts all right fur as I can tell, but I wuz in such a hell-awful fix that I'd kinder like ter be sounded erg'in. An' Doc, if you have occasion ter stop over night in these parts when you come, me an' the ole 'oman 'ud be powerful glad if you'd take the night with us."

Boozey Kanipe had been one of my most interesting patients and was now one of my best friends. He had suffered from chronic dyspepsia, the condition so common in the South Mountains, where vegetables and bread and other foods are fried in fat meat grease and where such grease is used in place of butter. Although he gave no history of regular drinking, his name was suggestive and I suspected alcohol to be at least partly the cause of Boozey's digestive troubles. His chief symptoms resulted from a nervous irritation of the heart, which at times manifested itself in the rapid beats of paroxysmal tachycardia. His condition had not been considered serious until a few weeks before I saw him, when he had had an attack of tachycardia while visiting a relative near Casar. A third-year medical student, at home for his vacation, lived nearby and came to see Kanipe. He pronounced the condition serious and said that sudden death was likely to occur from heart failure. The young man must have had an impressive manner for Boozey was sent home and put to bed and friends and relatives gathered to be present at what was expected to be his last illness. They stayed with him by day and took turns at sitting up with him at night, expecting the end to come at any moment.

This vigil was kept up for more than a week when Boozey, much improved by his long rest, began to chafe under the prospect of having to spend the remainder of his life in bed. His wife and family were obdurate, however, and would not allow him to get up. Finally, a compromise was reached and Boozey agreed to be taken to the new hospital at Rutherfordton for treatment.

Mt. Lebanon Church is on the main road from Sunshine to Rutherfordton, and at that time the churchyard was a popular camping place for mountain people going to the county seat. There was water and level ground and hitching places and feed troughs for the mules and horses. It was to this camping ground that I was called to see Boozey who was being taken to the hospital by wagon; I was to decide whether he was able to continue the trip that day and if he were likely to die on the way.

An examination convinced me that there was nothing organically wrong with his heart and that correct dieting and personal hygiene would do a great deal to improve his condition. After much persuasion I induced his wife and the attendants to allow him to get out of the wagon and they were all surprised when he walked over to my buggy in order to accompany me to my office, about three miles away. Further examination showed high gastric acidity, a condition easy to correct.

Boozey returned home the next day instead of going on to the hospital. An alkaline tonic and a change in diet brought quick results and made Boozey my friend and admirer.

• • •

Little Frank Freeman, a near neighbor and friend, knew the road to Huckleberry Gap and agreed to go with me; we started at sunup on Sunday morning. It was a typical autumn day such as is seen at its best in Western North Carolina. The hills were dark green in the early light but they took on a purple haze at the first touch of the morning sun; and light clouds of mist floated in the valleys. Smoke from kitchen fires went straight up to the sky, marking the position of homes in the valleys below us. The October air was chilly and showers of red and brown leaves were blown about us as we drove through the village of Sunshine and around the foot of Cherry Mountain and on over the hills, by Carson, Weast, and Marlin Peaks, towering majestically on the left as if to guard the valley of First Broad River.

• • •

Our first stop was at Wesley Fortenberry's, to see his wife, who suffered from rheumatism. Little Frank warned me against Wesley.

"Be careful, Doc, an' don't get 'im riled. He's as crazy as a loon, but he thinks he's a powerful smart man. His wife an' all the rest of his family air all right, but don't you start no argymints with Wesley. He'll talk yer ter death ef nothin' worse. Why, he will argy that Cherry Mountain is slippin' down an' 'at it ain't nigh as high as it use ter be. An' don't ever mention the railroad to 'im, Doc."

I found Wesley to be talkative but not at all aggressive.

"'Doc'", he said, as we came from the sick room, "afore ye go I'm a-goin' ter give you some advice. Get all yore docterin' done in these parts early. There's a-goin' ter be a terrible rough winter this year an' travelin' 'll be powerful hard. I looks fer a winter sech as we ain't had since the war — since the bad winter of '64, to be more exact. I was a-standin' guard at the Yankee camp at Salisbury that year an' it war so col' in the win' that my spine was chilled an' I ain't never been right since. I ain't over it yet. Follow my advice an' get yore docterin' done early. This winter's goin' ter be a caution ter what we're usen ter."

60

"Have you any particular reason for thinking this will be a rough winter?" I asked after I had thanked him for his advice.

"I have reasons a plenty fer knowin' it's goin' ter be a bad un'," he replied. "Have you noticed that there's lots of acorns this fall? That's a shore sign. An' ernother sign is the foggy mornin's of August. There'll be a snow fer ever' foggy mornin' in August. An' this past August I took 'count of the foggy mornin's an' there was thirty-three of 'em."

I promised to discuss the matter with him later since I must hurry on to other patients. A discussion as to the number of days in August might have ended in trouble.

As we drove away, Little Frank Freeman told me about Wesley's experience with the railroad, when he took a trip to Lincolnton years before. The railroad had just been built through Rutherford County and everyone was anxious to ride on the train. Among these was Wesley who went over to Bostic and boarded the train. When the conductor came round Wesley gave him fifteen cents, aiming to ride down to Ellenboro the next station. The conductor neglected to put Wesley off there and did not notice him again until the train had reached Lincolnton, fully fifty miles away. It took Wesley nearly four days to walk back home. He endured, so he said, many hardships, but the trip was the adventure of his life and he still talked of it, each time closing his narrative with the remark, "If the worl' is as big in ever' d'rection as she is down Lincoln way, gosh, but she's a whopper!"

●   ●   ●

We reached First Broad post office by eleven o'clock and were met by half a dozen patients who had come for minor complaints and for drugs. With these was Abe McFarland, who surprised me by saying that he had come to pay his doctor bill.

"Doc, I owes yer fer that trip ter see my boy when he had the pneumony fever an' the side pleurisy las' spring. I've done sol' my cross ties an' cotton an' as I hearn you war' passin' this side, I 'cided ter come out an' pay yer. Some o' the folks 'lowed 'at doctors don't 'spect ter be paid 'cept in November an' December, but I says ter 'em money's allus welcome ter a doctor jest like it is ter ennybody else. So, here I am."

I did not know the exact mileage from my home to McFarland's; so I asked him how much Dr. Avery, my predecessor, had charged per visit.

"Why, Doc Avery he use ter charge six dollars ever' time he come ter our house, but Doc Andrews, who use' ter live on Pea Ridge, he never charged but five dollars."

"Why did they make different charges when they both had the same distance to travel?" I asked.

"Well, Doc, it's this way. Me an' some o' the others discussed the matter at the time an' we decided 'at the best workman allus demands the highest wage."

It is needless to say that I charged Abe the higher rate for my visit; and I wondered if my services would have been more appreciated if I had made my charges larger.

• • •

From First Broad post office the main road winds up the river through fertile valleys for six or more miles to the settlement of Golden, with its church and mission school, and half a dozen stores in the center of twenty or more houses. Here we turned to the right into the Briar Creek road which leads to the source of the stream in the Huckleberry Mountains. We soon passed out of the level valley and into more hilly country, the road becoming narrower and rougher as we went along. The creek was crossed and recrossed and in some places the road went up the bed of the creek for many yards. But Little Frank knew the country well.

"There air erbout three mile of this, then we come out through Hard Bargain Gap past Little Huckleberry; — the road 'll be better from there ter Big Huckleberry."

"Have you ever been beyond Huckleberry?" I asked.

"On two 'casions, but not too fur in. Fact is, I've never been beyant Skiff Gaddy's Brandy Orchard. You've hearn talk o' Skiff, ain't yer, Doc?"

I had heard of Skiff whose reputation as a notorious "moonshiner", or illicit distiller, extended far and wide. Skiff, I had heard, was at present serving a sentence in the State penitentiary.

"Well, jest year afore last I went over to Luther Gaddy's — Luther is Skiff's boy an' lives at the Brandy Orchard since Skiff was sont up fer disturbin' 'ligious worship", continued Frank.

"What kind of country is it?" I inquired.

"Well I cain' say the country is so bad of itself from what I seed of it", reminisced Little Frank. "Hit's the folks what give it sech a powerful bad reperatshun. They're shore a wild lot, jest as wil' as bucks. You've seed them tallow-faced Briar Creek folks what never

62

shave an' don't get their hair cut but 'bout once a year an' who allus carry a rifle, ain't you?"

I nodded assent.

"To tell the hones' truth, that Briar Creek gang's got a college eddication 'side o' them what live beyant Huckleberry. They ain't no roads what you can drive over 'twix the Gap plum' on ter near Morganton an' they don't have post offices or schools. But they do a lot of blockadin' ter get rid of their corn crap, and the best mountain dew likker you can buy comes from them parts."

By three o'clock we reached the top of Little Huckleberry Mountain and drove on over the plateau lying between it and Big Huckleberry, which we could see in the distance, perhaps four or five miles away. Boozey Kanipe owned a farm in the level land between these mountains and we drove into his yard half an hour later. Besides the woman with the sick child there were at least thirty people waiting to see me, though not half of them came for medical attention.

"There's quite a bunch of 'em, Doc, though they ain't much the matter with some of 'em", explained Boozey after he welcomed us to his home.

"I put out word 'at you war comin' this side ter day an' I went further an' tol' 'em erbout what a good doctor you air an' how you saved me from a-goin' ter the horspittle whar's no tellin' what might a-happened ter me. It was a close shave I had."

"It was kind of you to tell them about me", I replied, "but the hospital is the best place to go when you are ill, especially if an operation is required."

"That may all be the truth, but it's the las' place ter go, 'cordin' to what I've hearn. Anyway, country folks don't thrive on docterin' what's done by town doctors an' nu'ses."

The first patient I saw was the little girl from "beyant Huckleberry". She was weak, anemic, poorly nourished, small for her age, had a protruding abdomen, and suffered from digestive disturbances. I now know that she suffered from hookworm disease, but I did not realize the cause of her illness at the time I saw her. My treatment was symptomatic and I gave full directions regarding food and fresh air and sunshine. These instructions I thought best to put in writing, before I learned the woman could not read.

"No, I ain't never had no call to do readin', as thar' ain't no mail route comes our side", she explained. "But yer can give me what you've writ down. We can allus get readin' done over in our valley.

63

I kno's a woman what lives lessen two mile below us what can read. Fact is, she does erbout all the readin' fer folks fer miles erroun'."

• • •

It was growing dark when I had finished with my last patient. Freeman and I had planned to "take the night" with Boozey, but while we were at supper there came a telephone call for me to go at once to see Big Jule Shelton's wife in the First Broad Valley three miles from Golden. The patient was described as being in a dying condition and I promised to start at once.

15

Carrying a Patient to the Hospital

IT WAS the night of the full moon, otherwise Little Frank Freeman and I would have found it difficult to drive down Briar Creek to Golden. Our horse had had a good rest and we reached the village by ten o'clock. Here we were awaited by one of the younger Shelton boys who had come to direct us through the valley to his grandfather's farm. We soon reached it and I could see that it was in keeping with Big Jule's reputation of being the richest man in Golden Valley. The house was much larger than the usual mountain home, while to the rear there must have been at least twenty barns, cribs, stables, and other out buildings.

On our way from Golden I had questioned the boy regarding his grandmother's illness.

"She's been ailin' off an' on fer more'n a year, but she's had three real bad attacks in less'n two weeks; an' ever' time the pain in 'er side an' shoulder gets wuss an' wusser."

"Has a doctor seen her"? I asked next.

"Not since 'er fust bad 'tack when Dr. Hunt from Casar come over ter see 'er, but, as he said, his med'sin' didn't do 'er much good; he recommended an operation. Uncle Jason Williams' been with 'er fer nigh on a week now, but 'er ailin' seems ter be erbove him an' he 'greed ter let Paw sen' fer you when we hearn you was a-ridin' in these parts."

"Old Mr. Williams is a relative of your family, isn't he?"

"Yes, he's my Aunt Sal's paw. You'll see the whole Shelton race when yer get thar'. Maw's been so bad that they're all come in ter be with 'er."

The Shelton "race", I decided, was a big one for we found the yard and house filled with men, women, and children; there were fully thirty people in the large room with the patient. As I entered I met and talked with Big Julius and his two oldest boys. I saw old Williams sitting by the hearth, but he did not speak or seem to notice my arrival.

The patient was a large old lady whose face was drawn with long continued pain. Her skin and eyes were jaundiced and the nature of the colic-like pains made it evident that her condition was due to gall-stones. It was also evident that surgery was necessary for her relief. I discussed the matter with the patient and she was willing to follow whatever course I thought best; she evidently realized that she couldn't live long in her present condition.

My plan was to make an ambulance out of a large covered wagon and carry the patient to the hospital in Rutherfordton. It would be easier for the patient, I thought, to begin the thirty mile journey at once. If we got started by midnight we should reach the hospital by the following noon.

I explained my plan to Big Jule and those who had gathered about the bed while I conversed with the sick woman. They had not understood what I was likely to suggest and when I mentioned the hospital a mild degree of pandemonium broke out. I had expected opposition but not in the marked manner in which it was expressed. There were anxious glances and shaking of heads, groans and muttered conversation; and this grew louder and louder, the patient's condition being forgotten. The climax was reached when old Jason Williams rose from his chair and came within the circle.

"No", he stated emphatically, "No! I'll never agree ter have Mandy took off ter no horspittle ter be cut up. That's bad advice. Doc Avery never took nobody from these parts ter a horspittle; he give 'em med'sin' an' all 'seases can be cured by med'sin' if yer get a doctor who knows his bus'ness. It's med'sin' Mandy needs — some'n ter ease 'er pains. If you'll furnish that an' get 'er easy so she won't throw-up so powerful bad, a pint o' sweet ile 'll make them gallstones pass. This docter warn't none too 'cessful with Little Preacher Jule's chaps, what both died, an' I know Big Jule ain't fool ernough ter let 'im take Mandy off ter town doctors who carve up folks jest ter 'speriment on 'em."

I raised my hand and asked for silence.

"I am surprised that you are all so thoughtless and care so little for Mrs. Shelton as to disturb her with all this noise. I am going to ask Mr. Jule and the two older boys here to come outside and discuss with me what is best for the patient. In the meantime, I must ask the rest of you to keep quiet. Mrs. Shelton is ill and has enough to bear without all this noise and foolish talk. Now, keep quiet or get out of the room!"

Something in my voice caused them to obey, for I was indignant at their thoughtlessness.

When I had the husband and older sons together I explained the patient's condition and did my best to show them that an operation was the only method of relief and that delay might prove fatal. I explained that a wagon could be prepared in such a way that the sick woman could make the trip in about as much comfort as she had at home and suggested that we start at once.

"It may be the best thing ter do, if you think thar' ain't no other way but ter take 'er ter the horspittle", said the old man.

"But Uncle Jason ain't never goin' ter agree fer Maw ter go ter the horspittle", said one of the boys.

"Listen to me", I said seriously. "You three are sensible men and I know you want your mother to get well. I am a doctor and it's my business to know about diseases. I have explained the situation to you and I have told you that in my opinion she can make the trip to the hospital if we start at once. It's up to you to decide whether you'll follow my directions or not. It's now twenty minutes until midnight. You can decide in that time; if you decide to allow your mother to stay at home and die, there's nothing more I can do and I will leave at twelve o'clock."

I left them and walked through the gate and down the lane as far as the watering trough. The full moon was high overhead and the valley was flooded with light. All was quiet and I debated whether or not I should leave the patient if they refused to take her to the hospital. After all, I might be mistaken—a narcotic would relieve the pain and the gallstones might be passed without an operation. I was undecided what I should do as I retraced my steps.

One of the boys came out of the house to meet me.

"Doc, we's decided ter let yer take Maw ter the horspittle, pervided you'll go thar' with us an' see that Maw is operated on in the right way an' that none of them town docters 'speriment on 'er. We's all of us mighty scared of the horspittle, but Maw says she knows she cain't go through ernother 'tack erlive. Uncle Jason won't give in and the gals air takin' on a-plenty, but Paw says he wants us ter do as you think best, since Boozey Kanipe an' some of the others give yer sech a good name. An' we had ter promise the gals they could go erlong with Maw in case she should die on the road."

•   •   •

The rapidity with which we made ready for our departure was surprising. Straw and feather beds were placed in the largest wagon and the patient was made as comfortable as in her own bed. One of the boys drove the wagon and I rode beside him so as to be near the patient. The two middle-aged daughters rode in the wagon at the side of their mother. They were both of a hysterical nature and I objected to their being so near the patient, especially since they had made such a scene when the hospital was first suggested. But as discussion meant waste of time I allowed them to have their way.

67

We made quite a cavalcade as we left the yard at one o'clock; in front of the patient's wagon was my buggy in which rode Little Frank and Big Jule, behind was another covered wagon with eight or ten near relatives; next was Uncle Jason Williams' buggy, followed by half a dozen men and boys on horses and mules. We left behind weeping women and grave-looking men who, I was convinced, never expected to see their relative return alive from the hospital.

We drove into the valley, crept past the village of Golden and on down the river to First Broad post office, where we made a short stop at three o'clock. The patient was none the worse for her journey; in fact she had slept part of the way and was in less pain than when she left home. Old Jason decided to leave us and drove away with the observation, "I 'spose you'll bury 'er at Mt. Lebanon."

At six o'clock we reached Pea Ridge where a stop was made to feed the horses and mules and get breakfast. I took the opportunity of going home to learn if I had other calls since my departure just twenty-four hours before.

An hour later I returned to the Cross Roads to find confusion. The two daughters were in tears and pleading with their father and brothers not to go on to the hospital. The patient was in very little pain and they were sure an operation was not needed. But I would not consider a delay and we started again.

Monday is wash day in the North Carolina hill country and a few miles from the Cross Roads we came to a house where the week's wash was already on the line. Seeing this one of the daughters remarked:

"Hain't that a master washin'? I bet some of their folks is down sick."

At Mack Freeman's near the Second Broad bridge, and at Johnny Ross' on Morris Creek, the family wash had also been completed. And at each place there was a recurrence of the exclamation:

"There's shore a big washin' out here. Somebody is shorely bad off!"

Finally at two in the afternoon we had passed through Rutherfordton and were going up the long hill upon which the hospital is situated. It had been wash day at the hospital, too, and the side lawns were covered with sheets, spread in the sun to dry. Here the girls exclaimed in unison:

"There's shorely somebody dead here!"

•   •   •

I felt a sense of relief when I turned the patient over to Dr. Biggs,

68

the hospital surgeon. She was weak and tired from her long journey and it was decided to delay operating for a few days in order for her to rest and regain her strength. But during her first night in the hospital there was a recurrence of acute symptoms and an emergency operation had to be done. Recovery was rapid and a few weeks later she had regained her strength and stopped to see me as she passed through Pea Ridge on her way home. Both she and her husband were hospital enthusiasts and loud in their praises of "town docters and nurses."

16

Chronic Pyrogastric Polydipsia

GRAHAM Parker had the reputation of being the biggest talker and the hardest drinker in the South Mountains. My friend Bud Green had told me about "Gra-ham", to give the local pronunciation of his name, long before I met him.

"He's the talkin'es' man in two states, an' it don't matter one bit whether he knows what he's talkin' erbout or not. Yer jest orter hear 'im. Why he'll hire one of Joe Devinney's boys ter plow 'is cotton ground an' pay 'im a dollar a day while he spen's his time walkin' up an' down the furrer behin' the boy, a-tellin' 'im all the news he's read in the Atlanty *Constertushun* erbout Huerty an' them other Mexican dagoes. An' as fer drinkin', Gra-ham keeps a jug of mountain dew under 'is bed all the time an' he don't get real sober but 'bout once a year. When 'is chaps gets the cotton picked in the fall he sobers up long ernough ter take it to Cliffside an' sell it; but the poor chaps don't ever see any of the money, tho' they've done gone an' picked the cotton."

During the summer and autumn I heard tales of Graham's sprees and the report that this year he was drinking more than ever before.

"He's been drunk now runnin' on ter five months", reported Green, "an' it's erbout time fer 'im to sober-up — the cotton crap's early this fall 'count of last summer's long dry spell. An', Doc, you'll shore have trubble with Gra-ham when he 'gins ter sober-up. Doc Avery allus 'ud spend the best part of a week with Gra-ham, a-holpin' 'im ter get straight. An' he's jest 'bliged ter have morphine at sech times."

"He'll get no morphine from me", I answered emphatically, for I had heard that Green himself was accustomed to go on sprees and I wanted him to understand my position as regards the use of opium in cases of drunkness. It was a joke in the community that on his last spell of drinking Bud Green had had his eyes examined and glasses fitted by a traveling optometrist; then when he sobered-up he found he could not see with the glasses.

The expected call from Graham Parker came on a foggy night during the latter part of October. It was past midnight when I reached his home and as I entered the room I could see that Graham's bed had been drawn before the fire which was roaring on the hearth. Graham was a small man, with reddish beard and gray hair; his face was intelligent but solemn, and he looked more like a country parson than the most notorious drunkard of the section. To my surprise, he was not talkative and did not seem to be very drunk. I shook hands, and asked of what he complained.

"Doc, you go right ahead an' make yore diagnosis. We'll talk later", was his reply.

"But I would like to know of what you complain and if you have any pain or particular symptoms — like indigestion, for instance."

"You go right ahead, Doc, an' make yore diagnosis; don't bother erbout me. Jest go ahead an' make yore diagnosis."

I asked further questions but received no answer except that I should "go ahead and make my diagnosis". I examined his chest and abdomen, but found nothing abnormal. I was somewhat puzzled as to what my next step should be when Graham ended my dilemma.

"Doc", he called in a low voice, "hit's my part ter pay fer yore visit an' it's yore part ter make the diagnosis. But I'll not be hard on yer this time; I'll help yer out, fer I know yer're young an' inexperienced bein' as how yer haven't been in practice fer long. I'll tell ye the trubble an' make the diagnosis fer yer this time. Come closer, I don't care fer the ole 'oman ter hear what's wrong with me".

I sat down again, drawing my chair closer to the bed.

"Doc", he whispered, "I'm jest on the eve o' gettin' on a drunk!"

"But I've been told that you've been drinking hard for the past six months", I informed him.

"No matter what you've hearn, I'm a powerful sick man. Ef yer don't give me some morphine I'm a-goin' ter die — it's the only thing 'at 'll quiet my nerves an' settle my stummick."

"I've got something that will do you more good than morphine. I'll give you a dose of it before I go."

"Doc, there ain't no need of yore experimentin' on me, fer nothin' 'cept a big dose er morphine has any effect on me. I've tried all the others. Get yore hyperdermic needle out, they's water already b'ilin' in that there skillet on the fire."

"You'll get no morphine from me", I asserted. "If you want the medicine I think you need, I'll prepare it for you, if not there's no need of my remaining".

"Doc, yer're mighty hard fer a young feller. I hearn tell that yer was mighty set in yore ways but I didn't believe ye was as bad as ye are. If you won't do nothin' ter holp a poor dyin' man in his distress, go ahead an' fix the stuff you'll gi' me."

Graham sobered on a bitter tonic, to which was added ginger and capsicum — a prescription designed to stimulate the stomach mem-

71

branes in a way similar to corn whiskey. Later, he reported to me that the mixture may have been better than nothing at all, but he told a different story to Bud Green. The medicine, he confided to Bud, had given him much trouble; it had a purgative effect and every time it acted he said he had to go to the river. Otherwise, he was afraid he'd set the woods on fire since the fall had been so dry.

•　　•　　•

It was ten years before I revisited the section. Many of my friends and ex-patients came to see me and one of the first to call was Graham Parker. I had already heard that he had reformed and was now a leader in the church at Mt. Lebanon.

"Doc, I've come ter see you perfeshunly as well as sociably", he announced. "C'u'd you an' me have a word conferdential-like?" We walked out into the yard.

"You may 've heard erbout me j'inin' up at Mt. Lebanon; that's one of the reasons I've come ter you. Since you moved from this settlement I ain't hardly needed a doctor 'til jest lately my stummick's been a-givin' trubble an' fer awhile I was real sick. I been 'tended by this new Doctor McDaniel from over erbout Forest City. Doc 'zamined me an' made 'is diagnosis an' he says I got the alcoholic gastritis. 'But Doc', I tells 'im, 'you shorely mus' be mistaken. I belong to the church. I may have the gastritis, like you say, but it cain't be the alcoholic gastritis'. But Doc sticks ter his diagnosis in spite of all I tells 'im an' says it may be the 'fects of my drinkin' in the past."

"Well, how can I help?" I asked.

"Now this is what I come ter you fer. I'd like fer you an' Doc McDaniel ter get tergether an' discuss my case, fer I know you air erquainted with my past an' you know I never was a drinkin' man. An', besides, it w'u'dn't look 'zactly right an' proper fer a leader in the church ter be havin' alcoholic gastritis, w'u'd it, Doc?"

I had to admit that it would not.

"Of course, I'll admit I use' ter drink a bit when I 'uz a young buck, but ter no great extent. An' we've had the proherbition here in North Caroliny fer more'n twenty years past. I 'members the fust likker law that was made. You c'u'dn't order but five gallons a month. Of course, I use' ter order the five gallon ever' month; an' it'd last me jest erbout a month. In fact, sometimes it would last a month.

"Then later on the law was changed an' you c'u'dn't order but a quart ever' two weeks. That's jest where I stopped foolin' with licker; — orderin' a quart at a time was jest too piddlin' a bus'ness ter pester with. Of course, I'll tell the truth an' say that I did sen' erway fer the quart ever' two weeks an' sometimes I'd order in the ole 'oman's name besides. But it warn't fer drinkin' purposes; it was because I wanted ter have a supply of them quart vials on han' in case one o' the chaps was ter get p'isened or snake-bit or somethin' like that.

"Yer can see fer yoreself, Doc, an' as yer already know, I ain't now an' never has been a drinkin' man. An' as I says ter Doc McDaniel, his diagnosis must be all wrong. It jest cain't be the alcoholic gastritis what ails me."

Graham noticed that I was becoming impatient.

"Jest one thing more, Doc, an' I'm through. I wants yer ter promise ter do me a favor fer ole times sake. I want yer ter see Doc McDaniel an' talk over my case with 'im. It'd relieve my min' a powerful lot if you doctors 'u'd make a diagnosis so I c'u'd tell the neighbors egzactly what ails me."

A few days later I happened upon Doctor McDaniel and we discussed the case of Graham Parker.

"Knowing his history as I do", I said "I'm sure your diagnosis is correct. In fact, I treated him ten years ago for acute alcoholism. But Graham has reformed and has deluded himself into believing that he has never been a drunkard. He feels that it doesn't sound right for a leader in the church to be suffering from anything caused by alcohol. I'm sure he'd appreciate it greatly if you gave his condition another name. He's very talkative, as you may know, and it would certainly give him great pleasure to be able to tell his neighbors the cause of his illness — and the bigger the name you give for his condition the better he will like it."

"I never thought of it in that way", said the Doctor, laughing, "but I am sure you are right. Suppose we say he suffers from chronic dyspepsia complicated by hyperchloridia?"

"Excellent", I replied. "South Mountain folks like to suffer from a complication of diseases."

"Or, we might say that his dyspepsia is complicated by a condition of chronic pyrogastric polydipsia", said McDaniel after a pause.

"Better still", I agreed. "With a few more phrases like that you'll have the most contented lot of patients in the South Mountains."

17

Doctoring the "Weed"

A S I have already mentioned, the life of a tenant farmer is a hard
one; it was especially so in the case of Jule Allison. The year
before I knew him had been an unusually dry one and crops had
been bad. After he paid his rent, food and clothing accounts, and fertilizer bills, his barns were empty and there was nothing left with which
to start the new year. More than this, he had rented a farm from a new
landlord in the hope of getting more fertile land and because he wanted
to be near a school. As a result, Jule was obliged to find work as a day
laborer to get corn for his mules. His own crop had to be left to the
women and boys, with what assistance he could give them on moon-
light nights. For food and clothing he was obliged to give his landlord
a lien for $200.00 on his share of all crops he might raise during the
year. By an old North Carolina law the holder of a crop lien had power
to take and sell enough corn, wheat, cotton, and other produce to meet
the debt. I am glad to say, however, that recent legislation protects
tenants from being bound by crop liens.

Jule Allison's landlord proved to be a hard one. He owned a
country store and charged exorbitant prices for the food and clothing
he advanced. In some instances as much as a third was added to the
cash price of supplies. And the clothing was all old stock and often
moth-eaten.

When Jule realized the unfairness of this arrangement he decided
to mortgage his two mules and secure supplies elswhere. But he
reckoned without his landlord. This man put in force a clause of the
agreement by which the lessee undertook to purchase his year's supplies
from the landlord. These agreements were made by a majority of the
landlords and a tenant had difficulty in securing good land without
making such a bargain.

My second professional call to the Allisons' came a few months
after the recovery of the little girl from dysentery. This time it was to
attend Mrs. Allison in a midwifery case; and the call came at night.

"Why haven't you notified me of your wife's condition before
now?" I asked Jule when he came out to meet me.

"Well, Doc, ter tell yer the truth, Carrie thought she'd try an' get
erlong 'thout a doctor this time, we air so fur in de't an' prospects fur
a good crap air so poor this year. But Carrie allus has sech a bad time

'at I jest made 'er let me sen' fer you, — but I c'u'dn't persuade 'er till the last minit."

I assured him of my willingness to give medical attention to his family at any time and take my chances as to pay.

When we entered the house I was surprised to see the main room lighted by a blazing fire, for it was a warm July night. Half a dozen women, including the patient, sat about the hearth. As I came up to the light I saw a large pot boiling on the fire.

"What's the idea of having a fire this hot weather?" I asked.

No one replied for at least a minute. Finally, Mrs. Allison spoke.

"Ask Maw Lawter", she said.

"Doc, its jest one of us ole women's idears", spoke up Miss Lawter boldly. "You mayn't hol' with sech, but we who's tried 'em know there's some 'n' in 'em."

"But what is boiling in the pot?" I inquired.

"Hit air a silver dollar", she replied. "Ter bile a silver dollar this way makes the labor easy."

"A silver dollar?" I asked incredulously, for I had never heard of such a custom.

"I know you don't believe in the vartue of sech, 'ca'se I can see yer a-smilin'," she continued; "but it's railly a good thing. By rights you orter have a dollar with the woman's birth-date on it ter get the best results. I use' ter have one with Carrie's birth-date on it, but once when we's hard-up I had ter trade it in at the store."

"Well, it certainly can't do any harm", was my comment.

"There's ernother thing, Doc", went on Miss Lawter. "We've been a-hearin' erbout yore new ways with cases sech as this; — how you make the woman strip to 'er gown an' wash an' go ter bed an' have clean sheets an' all sech things. Waco Loveland was a-tellin' us all erbout it an' it 'pears mighty strange seein' as how Doc Avery never use'ter make Carrie even take off her clothes at all an' he'd never even take the quilt from over her a single time."

"But go on an' tell it all", broke in Jule. "Didn't Waco say 'at the women what Doc 'tends all get up 'thout havin' child-bed fever?"

"Yes, he said that Maw", spoke up Mrs. Allison, "an' Waco orter know 'bout sech things 'ca'se he's a great un fer goin' ter sech cases. An' Preacher Francis Freeman's daughter-in-law, who Doc 'tended when he fust come to these parts, she tol' me with 'er own mouth 'at Doc's way's the best, an' she's had three young-uns. I allus has such a bad time with fever 'at I wants Doc ter manage this affair like he wants ter. So, yer jest shet up yore mouth, Maw."

The baby was born in a normal manner and both mother and child were in good condition when I left the next morning.

Jule followed me out to the buggy.

"Do you reckon Carrie'll get erlong all right?" he asked anxiously. "She's most allus sick an' she's had chile-bed fever rail bad two times."

There was no reason why the patient should have puerperal fever and I said so. And to reassure Jule I told him to feel free to send for me at any time if he felt that his wife or the baby was not making satisfactory progress.

On the fourth day I received an urgent call with the news that Mrs. Allison was very ill. I was genuinely surprised and feared the worst. Jule met me as before.

"Doc", he said, "Carrie's got the weed this time. I'uz a-feared she'd get it. She got erlong well till yestiddy, an' this mornin' she 'gun ter run fever."

Examination of the patient confirmed my worst suspicions. She was short of breath, had a high fever, a fast pulse, dry skin, and pains in all parts of her body. I instituted eliminative treatment —purgatives, forced fluids, diuretics, and hot packs. She reacted well and there was slight decrease in her temperature before I left.

I returned the next morning. To my surprise, as I drove up I saw Mrs. Allison sitting on the porch nursing the baby. Jule was with her and came to meet me.

"Doc, you're the best weed doctor we ever hearn of," he said enthusiastically. "Miss Lawter an' my Maw both say they never seed sech docterin' as you've done by Carrie. She's over her weed already, an' she had it rale bad. It allus took Doc Avery at least four days an' sometimes a full week ter break up the weed."

Not knowing what the "weed" might be, I contented myself with examining the patient. I could hardly believe my findings were correct. Her pulse, temperature, and respiration were normal, and except for weakness there was nothing wrong with her. I was much perplexed. The condition could not have been puerperal fever; — she had been too ill for recovery to be so rapid if the cause had been so serious.

My reputation as a successful obstetrician and, especially, as a "weed" doctor spread far and wide. And it was not until I visited

Cousin Dovie Freeman, about two weeks later, that I learned that "weed" is an engorgement of the breasts due to delayed lactation, — a condition usually brought on by the mother getting up too soon after confinement and catching cold.

In spite of it being only a fair crop year, Jule Allison was among the first to pay his medical bill in the autumn. I told him that I was glad he had made enough produce to "pay-out", but he made no response. It was some months before I learned that he had sold one of his mules to get the money.

18

Influence of the Moon

IN the spring we took a house at the Pea Ridge Cross Roads which had sufficient land for a large garden, and it was as an adviser on gardening that I came to know Fonzo B. Payne, who lived near Mt. Lebanon Church on the main road to Sunshine. I soon found that his advice was based mainly on how to read and follow the signs of the moon in order to obtain the largest crop yield. In the early days of March I consulted him about planting potatoes, for I had heard that potatoes should be planted on the dark of the moon — "endurin' the first dark nights of March," to be exact. In asking Fonzy about this, I pretended that I thought potatoes should be planted at night-time. He corrected this idea in as gentle a manner as possible, and then went on with the subject:

"Thar's nothin' ter plantin' taters on the dark o' the moon, Doc. Hit's jest an ole superstition. The moon railly ain't got n'airy a-thing ter do with it," I was surprised to hear him say. "Why, when I was jest a tincey chap I 'members hearin' my pappy say ter pay no mind ter moon signs when it comes ter plantin' yore 'taters. He says the time ter plant 'em is when the groun' is right; an' all my life I's foun' this ter be true. No, Doc, when yer come ter plant 'taters, the moon signs is nothin' but er old superstition; don't pay no 'tenshun ter 'em." Then his voice became low and earnest as he went on: "but, Doc, when yer plant yore beans, you'd better watch the moon signs."

From Fonzo B. and others I learned that the moon exerts an "awful" influence on farming and on life in general. The rule to be followed is to plant root crops, such as potatoes and turnips, on the dark of the moon, while crops such as corn, peas, or beans, which bear fruit above the ground, should be planted on the light of the moon. Peanuts are an exception and should be planted at full moon or the pods will not fill up.

Hogs should be killed when the moon is on the increase; meat killed on the dark of the moon will draw up and be tough when cooked, and will not yield much lard. And the moon was thought to have definite influence on cutting wood. Firewood cut on the increase of the moon will remain sappy and will just smolder and not give off heat. Also, shingles split or even laid on the roof during the increase of the moon will swell and curl up and cause the roof to leak.

The influence of the moon also extends to the human body, to babies as well as to adults. In fact, babies were believed to be born in most instances a day or so before or after the new moon; and if conception took place on the light of the moon the offspring will be a boy. If a wound or cut is made on the increase of the moon it will result in a big scar, while a cut sustained on the wane of the moon will heal rapidly and leave almost no scar at all. The signs of the moon must be watched when it comes to undergoing operations, even the pulling of a tooth. A tooth should never be pulled when the sign is in the head, since it would result in much bleeding and in a sore gum which is slow to heal.

Finally, Fonzo B. explained that the moon gives many indications of the kind of weather to be expected. A young moon with long horns is regarded as a kind of bowl which holds water. If the horns point upward dry weather will result, but if the points are down the moon is "spillin' water" and rain is sure to come. A halo about the moon indicates bad weather and rain is just as many days away as there are stars within the ring.

* * *

In addition to being a weather prophet and an adept on moon lore, Fonzo B. was a teller of tall tales. One of his most remarkable stories was about his adventure with a hoopsnake. And I was told that these mythical reptiles had been observed in the South Mountains by a number of observers. According to Fonzy's account, when he was quite a small boy he accompanied his father to Andrews' mill, on Puzzle Creek, a few miles from his home. They both walked and were carrying bags of corn to be ground into meal. Along the way they stopped to rest under a large oak tree. Boylike, Fonzy began to throw stones at a large rock which stood in the field below the road, and by chance a stone struck near where a hoopsnake was sleeping. The snake, being aroused, rose straight up on its tail and looked around, then, seeing the intruders, it took its tail it its mouth and began to roll up the hill toward them. Fortunately, they were on higher ground than the snake and this kept it from gathering speed as it rolled, thus giving Fonzy and his father time to dodge behind the big oak, which they did just as the snake reached them. By this time it was coming real fast and they jumped behind the oak so quickly that the snake rolled right into the trunk with such force that the sharp horn which grew out of the top of its head stuck into the bark and fastened it to the tree. Before the snake could pull its horn out, Fonzy's father killed it with a hatchet he had with him. They then fastened the snake's tail in a split stick and carried it with them to show the miller.

Several hours later, as they were returning home from the mill with their meal, they were surprised to see that the big oak tree was dying; already the leaves had withered and were dropping off, so deadly had been the poison the hoopsnake had injected into the bark through the sharp horn which grew out of the top of its head.

19

A Cure for the Hiccups

THE January day had been so rough, cold, and rainy, and the roads were so bad that it was after dark when I reached home from my calls. My telephone was out of order, but I was rather pleased at this since I would welcome a night free from calls. Soon after I had gone to bed and just as I was going to sleep I heard a horse approaching. My fears were realized — it stopped at the gate.

"Hullo! Hullo! Air yer at home, Doc?" shouted a voice.

"Yes. Who are you? What's wrong?"

"Sudie May is much wuss an' Cort says ter tell you ter come at once."

I got out of bed hoping to learn enough to justify me in sending medicine instead of driving four cold miles over bad roads to Cort Littlefield's. But the messenger had not waited and when I reached the door the sound of the horse's hoofs was growing indistinct.

There was nothing to do but go; so I dressed, gathered my buggy robes, lighted my lanterns, and started for the barn to hitch-up the horse. The thermometer registered below freezing as I passed down the porch, and a drizzling rain was falling and freezing on the ground. With a lighted lantern under the buggy robes to keep me warm, I started. My only consoling thought was the fact that Cort Littlefield was one of the few who always paid the doctor at each call.

Sudie May Littlefield, a nervous girl of twenty-three, had been ill for years, according to the history I gathered at the time of my first visit to the family. Her ailments had been many and varied, but I had been called to see her for some kind of digestive upset. My treatment not only failed to bring relief, but the symptoms became more complex and indefinite. On my last visit two days before I had decided that she was suffering from hysteria, pure and simple. This was also the opinion of many of the neighbors who called her sickness the "hippo", declaring that she was "hippoed".

It was past midnight when I reached the Littlefield home. As I drove up I saw that the large two-story house was fully lighted, and on coming to the porch I could see through the window into the patient's room. A large crowd was gathered about the open fire and around the bed, all talking in muffled tones. A preacher was standing by the patient's side, reading from his Bible.

General Littlefield, an uncle of the sick girl, came out to meet me.

"Doc, I'm a-feared you've come too late. Sudie May got wuss erbout dark and started hiccupping. This has kep' up and has weakened her an' she has been too low ter speak for more'n an hour. She's sinking fast."

"Who are all the folks"? I asked.

"They are kinfolks an' neighbors. Sudie May had 'em sent fer so she c'u'd tell 'em good-bye afore she passes on. That's Parson Elbert Toney a-readin' the Bible. He was visitin' over to Jule Allison's place and heerd of our trouble an' come over ter help."

The crowd moved back from the bed as I entered the room. The patient was lying flat on her back, hiccoughing for dear life. The bed covering was turned down and her gown had been opened at the front in order that she might get more air. She did not speak when I addressed her. I felt her pulse — it was normal; I counted her respiration, that was normal, too: I examined her heart and found nothing wrong. I was now sure of my diagnosis.

Being nettled by having to make an unnecessary cold drive, I decided upon heroic measures. Going out on the porch to the water shelf, I brought the bucket half filled with water and mush ice, and dashed it with some force upon the patient's bare chest. The crowd held their breath and consternation was written upon their faces; they were aghast at the procedure.

But the silence was only for an instant. The girl sprang up with a scream and rushed to the fire pronouncing fierce anathemas on a doctor, who, she declared, had no more sense than to try and murder a helpless sick person. But the hiccoughing had stopped!

It took some time to get her quieted, but when she was warm and dry and had changed her clothes, it became generally realized that she had not been seriously ill. The visitors left, the family were reconciled to the treatment, and the minister was heard taking off his boots in the room overhead.

20

Assorted Interesting Cases

THERE was no end of interesting cases which came under my observation during my stay in the South Mountains or of interesting happenings in connection with their treatment. A most curious and humorous manifestation of mental illness was the case of Uncle Decatur Nelson. This old gentleman, well in his eighties, had a slight stroke with partial paralysis from which he had practically recovered. But mild mental symptoms persisted. The most characteristic of these was his belief at times that he was a coffeepot. He would sit nodding in his big armchair, when all at once he would straighten up, place his right hand on his hip somewhat like the handle of a coffeepot, and then hold his left arm out, half flexed like the spout. Maintaining this position he would begin to make a low noise like the simmering of a heated coffeepot. This noise would gradually become louder and louder, finally to resemble the sound of boiling water; and this would keep up until Aunt Hallie, his wife, would take hold of his right arm and go through the motion of pouring out the coffee. Then Uncle Decatur would relax and doze off until the manifestation would be repeated several hours later.

• • •

Mrs. Hamp Higgins had "the hippo" (hysteria) and, although she had been treated by doctors in four counties she had not improved. In fact, she had become an A-1 nuisance to all these medical men. Fortunately for me, just before I came to the district she found relief in treatment by an advertising magnetic healer (that is what he called himself), who was located out in Missouri. Professor Larson, the healer, after receiving a fee of $50.00, sent explicit directions to the patient. Treatments were given twice a week at specified times; at the appointed hour the patient was directed to lock herself in her room and at the same hour the doctor in his office out in Missouri would concentrate on her case. At such times he pretended to send out magnetic waves suitable to the patient's condition. Mrs. Higgins declared that she could feel these waves enter her body; as a result, she was cured of her nervous symptoms — at least temporarily. It was difficult to understand how such treatment could be effective until a report from the American Medical Association's Council on

Nostrums and Quackery stated that each of Professor Larson's patients was provided with a jar of salve, composed mainly of vaseline and red pepper, to rub on the arms and legs just before the treatment hour. This, it was explained, was to make the patient's body more receptive to the Professor's magnetic waves.

•   •   •

My reputation as a clever doctor was enhanced by the successful treatment of old Mr. Caleb Lovelace, who lived near Sunshine. Years before, Caleb had been to Baltimore and while there had been treated at the out-patient clinic of the Johns Hopkins Hospital. The medicine he received had restored him to complete health, though the cause of his ill-health could not be ascertained from his account. Later he had been examined and treated by doctors in all the nearby towns in the hope of finding one who would be able to diagnose his case correctly and prescribe the same medicine he had received at the Hopkins Hospital. Also, he had written to the Hospital but for some reason his record could not be located and he was still without this "wonder medicine," as he called it.

When I located on Pea Ridge, Caleb was one of my early patients. After listening to his long history in detail and then examining him, I came to the conclusion that he was in fair health. This opinion, however, didn't satisfy him, so I gave him a bottle of *Liq. Triplex* (Iron, Quinine, and Strychnine), a bitter tonic much in use at the time. This proved to be the medicine he had been given at the Hopkins Clinic and my fame as a well qualified doctor was spread by the Lovelace family.

Later, when I treated one of the grandchildren, I inadvertently left a thermometer at the home. Caleb 'phoned to tell me that I had gone off and left my "fever gauge" and that he was keeping it for me.

•   •   •

Many of the mountain people held strange ideas regarding doctors and medicine. One winter day I made a long trip to Dysartsville, in McDowell County, to see an old lady in consultation with a doctor from Marion, the county seat. As I was entering the village I was hailed by a small strange-looking man who ran out to my buggy and asked in a loud whisper:

"Air you a specialist?"

I replied that I claimed to be no more than a general practitioner. At this he looked disappointed and explained:

"If you'd been a specialist, I'd have had you stop and see my wife."

In the care of typhoid fever cases very little medicine is needed, good nursing being the most important part of the treatment. But in the South Mountains a doctor was expected to give medicine and the patient and his family were disappointed if medicine was not supplied. Because of this I used boiled water, colored red, as routine in my typhoid cases and found it went far toward satisfying the family as regards medicine; and, as it was prescribed to be given in tablespoonful doses in a full glass of water, it insured the patient's getting enough water. As I had good luck with such cases, their recovery was usually ascribed to the "red fever mixture." However, on one occasion when a boy was sent on muleback for more than a dozen miles to my office to get a bottle of this red fever mixture, I could not help but feel guilty of deception — or something.

●   ●   ●

And I shall never forget the instructions given by old Mrs. Tollie Huntsinger to her daughter-in-law when the girl was in labor: "Honey, shet yore mouth, hold yore breath, grit yore teeth, clinch yore fists, grin, and enjoy it!" The girl followed instructions as best she could, but after the baby was born she declared that "ef there's enny more black haw tea drunk at this house, Calvin Huntsinger 'll have ter do the drinkin' of it!"

21

Finances

ON October 6, 1912, I married Miss Zillah Howe, a nurse I had known at the James Walker Memorial Hospital in Wilmington, N. C. Soon after our marriage we rented a house on Pea Ridge where the road from Sunshine to Rutherfordton crossed the road from Bostic to Brittain. The house had seven rooms, conveniently built on one floor, with verandahs at the front and back and a well near the kitchen door. With the house there were two acres of land, barns and stables. We were surprised that the rent was only $3.00 per month. This low rate, we reckoned, was due to the small amount of land on which a farm family could not earn a living. And there were few people except farmers in the country. But our friend Bud Green did not view the matter as we did.

"How much rent do yer pay fer this place?" he asked.

"Three dollars a month."

"Three dollars a month", he exclaimed. "You don't mean ter say that Will Reid charges yer three dollars a month for this little place. Why, there's hardly two acre of land. It's a damned hold-up; he's never charged more'n two an' a half fer this place before. It ain't right that he sh'u'd charge you more jest beca'se you're strangers to these parts. I'll give him a piece of my mind, I will, when I see 'im next."

We found the cost of living to be very low on Pea Ridge; but we soon learned that a doctor's cash income was small. The country, being mountainous and hilly, with rough roads and great distances to be traveled either on horseback or in a buggy made it impossible to visit patients oftener than was absolutely necessary. The people were poor and many mountain families lived on small farms and produced their own foodstuffs; such people handle little cash during an entire year. Because of this, in many instances, ridiculously low fees had to be charged for long tiresome journeys to inaccessible places where skilled medical or surgical work was performed. A further handicap was the fact that cotton, the only money crop, produced a small yield in this hilly section; and, of greater importance to a doctor, this crop was gathered and marketed in the autumn. This meant that doctor bills, like store and other bills, must await payment until the cotton had been sold.

But the honesty, hospitality, and generosity of the people in many ways compensated for their lack of ready money. We had hardly

"Rough roads and great distances to be traveled either on horseback or in a buggy made it impossible to visit patients oftener than was absolutely necessary."

settled in our new home when visitors began to call. The season had been favorable for sweet potatoes and each visitor brought a bushel bag or even more as a kind of wedding present. We stored these potatoes in a spare room, but it was soon full and the barn had to be used for the overflow.

It was not necessary for us to have a vegetable garden, for nearly every caller brought fruit or vegetables or eggs. And when visits were made to the sick, it was usual to find the buggy filled with foodstuff when I started for home.

As a result of these conditions we lived comfortably but, like our neighbors, we were always short of cash. Buggies, saddles, harness, clothing, drugs; all these had to be bought on credit. We watched the cotton crop with as much zeal and longed for it to be bounteous with as much ardor as the farmers themselves.

The spring had been cold and rainy and cotton was late in being planted; the summer was hot and dry, even too dry for cotton which requires hot nights for its best growth. Finally autumn came and the "me'jum crap" was gathered; then people began paying their medical bills. The more prosperous brought money; others, whose cash had been taken for fertilizer bills, brought part money and arranged to pay the remainder in corn or fodder or wood or hams. Still others, less fortunate ones, having no cash brought calves and pigs, or canned fruit and vegetables, and some brought beautifully made quilts and bed-spreads. One poor widow, barely able to support herself and children on her rocky farm, sent six pairs of heavy woollen socks, home-knitted and bright red in color, although I had not sent her a bill. Barney Beam, an old bachelor, brought me a scarf pin made from a large nugget of native gold, in part payment of his bill. (This recalls an interesting custom of the Golden Valley section. When a couple decided to get married, it was customary for the man to pan enough gold for a wedding ring, after the manner gold was mined in the South Mountains up to the time of the discovery of gold in California. In Barney's case, the lady changed her mind and married someone else and the gold was made into the stick pin which became one of my prized possessions.) Everyone tried to pay to the best of his ability and there was little or no effort to shirk debts; and by the end of November the great majority of my clientele had arranged their payments.

•   •   •

It was at this time that Bud Green paid us one of his periodic visits.

88

"Doc, I've come ter give yer some advice erbout collectin', ef you don't min' takin' advice. When Doc Avery was ridin' these parts I'd allus help 'im in the fall. Have the folks been comin' in ter settle as they sh'u'd?"

"Yes, they have done fairly well," I replied.

"But thar's some you'll have ter go after jest like Doc Avery use' ter do. The only way ter get 'em is fer you ter sen' 'roun' a two-hoss waggin an' have it go from house ter house an' gather up corn an' fodder an' shucks an' sech ruffness an' meat and other food truck."

"That might be a good plan", I agreed, for a number of families had promised to pay in produce but had no way of delivering it.

"Yes, an' I knows the country well. Ef you sh'u'd like I c'u'd take my big waggin an' a couple of the boys an' visit them what owes you. I can gorontee I'll fotch in the stuff fer you."

Arrangements were made for Green to make a tour of the different districts to collect produce in payment of medical bills.

"Thar's jest one other p'int, Doc", said Bud as he was ready to leave, "an' it's a important p'int. Endurin' this pay season you sh'u'dn't wear sech good clothes, lessen folks sh'u'd come ter think 'at you don't need money. Why, ever' fall Doc Avery 'ud put on 'is ole bagged an' patched suit an' get 'is ole rattly buggy an' use 'is ole harness what was all tied up with strings and pieces of wire; and Doc was a monstrous fine collector. Even ole Nob Lowrance, who has the name of never paying a debt, paid 'im once. Nob come out ter see what was the trubble when Doc's buggy broke down in front er 'is house; an' when he seen how ragged Doc was an' what a pore buggy he was a-drivin', he actually paid Doc two dollars on 'is account."

Green was highly successful and filled our barns with corn and fodder, our smokehouse with meat, and the stables and barn lot with calves and pigs, to say nothing of the chickens and other fowls he brought. He also brought miscellaneous articles such as an old-time cap and ball revolver, and a set of obstetrical instruments which had been left in a mountain home some forty years before by an old Dr. Nabors.

There was only one glaring case of refusal to pay. Green reported this as follows.

"It war that onery Calvin Fortenberry, who's a low-down cuss, any-how, an' one you w'u'dn't 'spect no better from, seein' as how he come from over Briar Creek way. He ain't intendin' ter pay yer, Doc, for he's movin' up ter nigh Dysartsville in McDowell County at the end of the year. He had plenty of fodder but w'u'dn't 'low me ter take any of it. He said his wife's brother holp raise the crap an' he c'u'dn't move any of it till the boy come back from Marion whar' he's 'tendin' court. He promised ter leave a 'fodder pole' fer you, but you needn't count on it, fer I don't b'lieve he means ter pay yer. I'm goin' over that way endurin' Christmas week an' I'll look in an' see if he leaves anything."

We did not see Green again until after the New Year. He came to give a report on his visit to the Fortenberry place.

"He'd done moved when I r'ached thar. A man named Ike Mitchum lives at the place this year. I axed 'im erbout the pole of fodder Calvin war ter 've left and Ike started ter laugh; an' he laugh an' he laugh. Finally, I axed, 'What in the name of Gawd ails yer?' Then he took me out ter the barn lot an' showed me a tall fodder pole that was high ernough ter 've hel' nigh on ter four hundred bundles, but thar' war jest three bundles tied on ter the tip-top of it. Ike said Calvin had tole all the neighborhood 'bout how he war playin' a good joke on the doctor, a-leavin' a fodder pole like he said he'd do, 'cause he hadn't said how many bundles of fodder there'd be on it."

"Calvin and Ike have rather a peculiar sense of humor", was my comment. "What did you tell Ike?"

"I tole 'im ter sen' word ter Calvin that the docter said if that twelve dollars warn't paid soon he'd tell what he knows erbout Calvin a-makin' licker over on Briar Creek. I 'low that 'll give Calvin some'in' ter think erbout, even if yer don't know nothin' erbout what he done on Briar Creek."

Calvin Fortenberry was more frightened by the message than Green thought he would be. I chanced to meet him in Rutherfordton during the next fortnight. He was voluble in his greetings.

"Doc, I'm shore glad ter see you. In fac', I was a-'lowin' ter go home by Pea Ridge jest a-purpose ter pay that twelve dollars I owes you. I tho't I'd a been by that way afore now or I'd a writ' an' sent yore money."

"I thought you were going to leave a fodder pole to pay me", I replied.

"Well, I did aim ter leave yer a pole but jest at the last minute I got a chance ter sell the fodder an' I know'd you'd rather have the money, so I sol' the pole."

He paid the twelve dollars.

"Doc, thar's ernother matter I'd like ter talk ter you erbout. I'd a little rather nobody heered us. S'posen we walk out ahind the court 'ouse."

He led the way through the "bone yard", or rows of horses and mules tied to the scores of hitching racks, where the court-day crowd of horse traders were gathered. We went over behind some warehouses, away from the crowd.

"Doc, I'd like ter have yer tell me exzactly what yer knows erbout my makin' licker up on Briar Creek", he whispered in a nervous voice.

"Nothing at all", I laughed. "That was just one of Bud Green's jokes in return for your leaving me a fodder pole with only three bundles on it."

He searched my face anxiously.

"Is that the Gawd's truth yer're tellin', Doc? War it only a joke?"

He became indignant when I assured him that I knew nothing whatever of his life in the Briar Creek section.

"That damned Bud Green! Ter think of 'is playin' me sech a joke, the damned rascal! An' me intendin' ter pay you all the time. You know'd I'd pay you, didn't yer, Doc?"

His tone was not convincing. I felt sure that I would never had been paid except for Green's practical joke. However, I replied that I now had my money and that the matter was closed.

"But, all the same, it war a dirty, low-down trick of Bud Green, when I was intendin' ter pay you all the time", were his parting words.

· · ·

By the opening of spring the crops had all been marketed, including the cord-wood and cross-ties which had been cut and hauled to the railroad during the winter months; and the farmers were starting their planting. It would be eight or nine months until another "pay season". All debts, doctor bills and others, had been paid to the best of each family's ability. Unpaid accounts would have to remain over another year, and their final payment would depend upon the yield and the price of the next cotton crop.

It was a suitable time to make an inventory; but the inventory left my wife and me disappointed. Our barn was filled with corn and horse feed and our smokehouse with a year's supply of meat and canned fruit and vegetables. The surplus had been sold along with the livestock we had received in payment of medical bills. Our buggies and harness had been paid for and also the bills for clothing and drugs, but we had no cash surplus and debts must be incurred for a new supply of drugs and for another horse. There was no money for books or magazines.

The future did not look promising. We realized that the people were honest and willing to pay for medical service, but that the amount they could pay a doctor was not sufficient to meet his expenses for travel, drugs, instruments, and living. And we saw no hope of my ever being able to attend the meetings of medical societies or take post-graduate courses; we could not even subscribe for the medical journals I wanted. And these things are essential to the practice of medicine in an efficient manner.

What should we do? Should we try our fortune in some town or more prosperous country district? Prosperous districts were already supplied with doctors and in case we moved to such a place it would likely take months to build up a practice. The reason I had come to the South Mountains was that I had no money for living expenses while a practice was being started.

Our dilemma was ended a few months later by an offer from the Rockefeller Sanitary Commission for me to become a field director in the hookworm campaigns they were conducting in the State.

22

Leaving the South Mountains

IT was in April that I accepted the offer of the Rockefeller Sanitary Commission to become a member of their field staff then engaged in public health work in the Southern United States. We had to close my practice and leave Pea Ridge in a month — on May 20th, to be exact. This last month was a very full one. The news that we were leaving spread rapidly and we found that the people were astounded at our decision. Folks came to us from all parts of the district around, from the South Mountain country, and even from "beyant Huckleberry". They wanted to learn why we were leaving. They tried to persuade us to stay and when they found they could not they arranged for the payment of their medical bills, while some came to get a last bottle of some 'tonic' which had been effective.

Among our visitors was Big Sam Biggerstaff, a well-to-do farmer from near Sunshine, to whose house I had never been called.

"Doc", he said with great earnestness, "we's all hearn that you air ter leave us. Thar' isn't none of me an' my crowd never been sick since you've been ridin' in these parts, but we know of yore repertashun an' the whole country-side is a-grievin' beca'se of yore goin'. Me an' Bill Jack McMurray talked the matter over with some of t'others an' we decided I sh'u'd come an' ax yer man ter man fer what reason you air a-leavin' us. We all know 'at you get a-plenty of ridin' ter do, so it can't be 'ca'se yer don't keep busy. Is it beca'se the people won't pay you? Or don't Mis' Zillah like us country folks?"

"Why no, Mr. Sam" I said, "that's not it, I can assure you of that. She loves the whole country."

"Well, some of the women folks", said Sam, "reasoned that she bein' from furrin parts, mebbe she don't enjoy livin' in this hill country. We hope it ain't that ca'se our own women folks shore do like yore wife an' she seems jest like one of our own country-raised girls."

Then my wife came up and together we assured him of our very real love for the country and the people. We had never lived among better folks. And as for the bills, why nearly everyone had paid. He was even then persistent, so I explained more fully why I was ceasing to be a 'riding doctor.'

"We both know", I said, "that we shall never find better people to work among than these right here. But there's a new branch of doctor's work now called public health work. Instead of physicking sick folks, a public health doctor spends his time keeping towns and communities and whole big districts well. His work is to teach the people how to live and eat right so they won't get sick, and advise them about the best way of building houses and to keep their homes clean so that diseases won't spread and a big part of his business is to see that laws against the spread of the catching diseases are enforced. I am sure keeping people well is a much more important job than patching up diseased individuals who are in bad health because of their wrong habits of living."

All this made little impression. A long life among people who, if not always ill, were never really very well or no more than 'tol'able' rendered him unable to think of a place that did not need perpetual drenching.

"Yes, but it all seems so onpractical, Doc", was his comment. "How do you expect ter make a livin' at that kind o' work? People ain't a-goin' ter pay you fer jest tellin' 'em how ter keep well; folks is got ter get med'sin an' they won't paternize a doctor who don't give it."

"In other States and in the eastern part of North Carolina", I explained, "there are public health doctors who are paid by the counties out of the taxes. I only hope Rutherford County may have such a doctor some day."

Big Sam shook his head.

"It may be all fer the best", he said sadly, "but it won't be in yore or my day an' generation when the folks in these parts 'll 'gree ter be taxed ter pay a doctor ter go 'roun' an' him never a-givin' of drugs at all. The Bible says 'Cleave ter the ancient landmarks'; an' doctors have allus been doctors, so fur as I ever heared, an' not jest gabbers. I shore wish yer well, but I'm a-feared you're makin' a mistake; you, sech a good homey doctor, a-runnin' after sech new-fangled notions."

Perhaps after all I did deserve his compliment of being a good homey doctor, for as the time grew near for us to leave we found our regrets at having to go grew still greater, and packing was really a sorrowful task. When it was done and the time came for us to go we arranged for Bud Green to haul our trunks and boxes to my father's house in the southern part of the county, and he brought his wagons to begin loading the night before. He explained why.

"Doc, I thought I'd better bring these waggins eroun' an' get 'em packed ergin the coming of dark, 'ca'se thar'll be sech a crowd here ter-morrer a-sayin' goodbye that it'll be hard ter get anything done."

This was what I was afraid of. It might be that to them our going was a kind of funeral, and does not everyone come to a funeral?

94

"Why, we've already been around and said goodbye to almost everybody", I replied, "and we're to leave by ten o'clock tomorrow, stop at Zeb Freeman's for dinner, and go on to Rutherfordton in the afternoon."

Bud Green smiled grimly.

"Lucky if yer get away as you plan", he said. "You ain't erquainted with these folks even yet, Doc. You've said goodbye ter them, but they ain't said goodbye ter you. They all know they won't ever get ernother doctor in these parts, that's why they hates so bad ter see you an' Mis' Zillah go. Thar' may come some uppity town doctor, but thar' ain't likely to come a common country doctor like you that is jest home folks to us all."

Bud was right. We may have said goodbye to them but they wanted to say goodbye to us. Friends and neighbors, and some we did not know, came early and remained until we had gone. The first to come was Jule Allison in his two horse wagon; he brought his wife and baby, two other children, his mother, and mother-in-law. He was followed by Babers, Longs, Holifields, Thornes, Freemans, Toneys, Hardins, and many others from representative families. The men stood about the yard, most of them chewing tobacco in silence, while the women sat with the children on the porches and dipped snuff. It was a holiday to them but surely not a very cheerful one. From time to time we left our packing to go out and speak to them. They talked but little; Wesley Fortenberry, the weather prophet, was one of the few to ask questions.

"Exzactly whar' is it you air headed fer when yer get started from here, Doc?"

I told him something of preventive medicine and of my hope of becoming a county health officer when I had finished my work with the Sanitary Commission. He failed to understand.

"But exzactly ter what pertic'lar place air you a-goin'?" insisted Wesley.

"To the eastern part of this State and later I may be sent to the West Indies", I answered.

"Never hearn of sech places", said Wesley. "Air they as fur off as Lincoln? I's been down that side."

"Much further than Lincoln", I replied with a smile.

"Gosh! But they must be a good step erway", was his final comment.

Graham Parker was a late arrival; he was sober and as talkative as ever. Among the things he told us was that he and his wife had named their new baby Mal Benjamin in honor of Dr. Mal Andrews, one of my predecessors, and myself. A little girl, born two years before, had been named Halley in honor of the visit of Halley's comet, so, of course, I expressed great pleasure at the compliment. It was something to be bracketed equal with a comet.

In reply to Graham's questions as to where we were likely to go, I mentioned Trinidad as one possible place. Probably besides ourselves he was the only person in the crowd who knew it existed. To my surprise he even placed it.

"Trinidad! That's nigh on ter Venezuweely, ain't it, Doc?"

"Yes, close to South America, Graham."

"My advice, Doc, is that you'd better stay erway from them thar South Ameriky countries. I's been a-readin' erbout 'em in the Atlanty *Constertushun;* they're jest as likely ter have a revolution at one time as ernother. You go thar' an' jest erbout the time yer get settled they'll have a revolution; an' you might have ter run off an' leave yore diagnosis", he said as he pointed to my microscope.

• • •

At last the time came for us to start on our journey. We went around and shook hands with everyone and said goodbye to them all individually. The women cried and the men stared at us mournfully, but all wished us God-speed.

I had not realized until that very morning how much I liked these people. At moments I had to combat the thought that a life-time spent in the South Mountains country would not be half wasted. In fact, it might be just as attractive and just as productive of good as anything I might achieve in the greater field of public health. As we drove off I said as much to my wife and was glad when she asked,

"Don't you reckon we could somehow change our plans and stay here after all?"